Skiing Without Fear

– for Beginners, Intermediates & Experts –

How to Overcome Your Fears, Build Your Confidence, and Improve your Skiing through NLP, Visualisation and Hypnosis

By Leighton Ellis.

You can join the "skiing without fear" forum, download the eBook or audio versions of this book, along with any additional notes, revisions and other good stuff at:

http://www.skiing-without-fear.com

First Published in the United Kingdom July 2010 by Eroica Ltd.
Company No. 3457609

ISBN: 978-0-9565127-0-3

Table of Contents

Index of Exercises

Preface

A little bit about the author

Originally from the United Kingdom, I now live in Chamonix valley in France – a 'Mecca' for outdoor adventure sports - drawn by my passion for paragliding and skiing.

Together with my darling wife, Helen, we run a ski in, ski out chalet in Les Houches at the entrance to Chamonix valley – the family-end of Chamonix valley with lots of tree-lined blue and red pistes. We receive guests at all levels of skiing ability, thus it is the perfect environment to study fears and skiing, and how to apply NLP and Milton Erickson's hypnosis techniques to build your confidence and improve your skiing.

I do not think of NLP as the 'be-all' and 'end-all' of techniques to 'cure' all phobias and fears – also simply reading from a book does not have nearly the effectiveness as working one-on-one with someone experienced in NLP techniques. However, I believe that most of these techniques can be easily learnt and applied *by you* to help you overcome your own fears and build your confidence skiing.

I believe that NLP and visualisation have a number of effective techniques you can use to help you master your fears, and build your confidence. Consequently, I think of this book as merely a conduit to help you learn some of those techniques, and if you apply those techniques appropriately to yourself, you will gain mastery over your fears, anxieties and distresses related to skiing.

A note on the language and grading systems

As I am located in France, I apologise to my North American readers if you struggle a little with some of the language used which will inevitably have an Anglo-French influence, especially on terminology.

Moguls = bumps
Ski piste = ski trails

Also, the way the ski trails are graded is very different in Europe – and the two scales are very difficult to relate. In Europe, the most you can expect is that the grading system reflects the relative steepness of the slope within that actual resort itself.

European grading:

- Green – very easy

- Blue – easy

- Red – intermediate

- Black - difficult

American grading:

- Green – very easy

- Blue – easy

- Single black diamond = roughly equivalent to Red/Black in Europe

- Double black diamond = roughly equivalent to Black in Europe

- Triple black diamond

Introduction

"NLP is an attitude and a methodology that leaves behind a trail of techniques." – Richard Bandler.

For me, skiing is one of the most amazing activities that a person could ever experience.

The idea is simple: strap two planks of wood to your feet and slide down a slope covered in snow. Far from the original concept where you would have to hike up the hill first, skiing is now a relatively easy and safe pastime, with high-speed lifts whisking you to the summit peaks and high-technology skis that are easier to control and steer with safe, reliable binding systems designed to protect your ankles, knees and legs.

Yet, despite all these wondrous technological advances, whether you are a beginner, intermediate, or advanced skier, there is still one piece of firmware that can chronically hold you back: your own brain.

More specifically, as a human animal, we still have our basic *"fight-or-flight"* responses that were designed to protect us when we were chasing lions on the prairie. However, and unfortunately, this mechanism can sometimes get in the way of us being able to operate at our peak performance in all kinds of situations – one of these being on skis, or a snowboard.

What this book aims to do is to provide is a methodology and valid techniques to enable you to produce your peak performance *every time* you hit the slopes.

Sure, you *will* need to learn some *technical* skiing skills from a professional – for example: you need to learn how to snowplough if you've never skied before, to learn how to do a parallel turn once you've mastered your basic snowplough turn, how to do jump turns if you want to ski gullies or couloirs.

This book does not come close to being an instruction manual on *"how to ski"*, nor is it intended to.

11

Instead, think of it as an instruction manual on *"how to control your brain so it doesn't hold you back when you are skiing"*.

This is something which can affect us all: beginners, intermediate and advanced skiers alike.

Whilst advanced skiers will not have the same *level* of fear given the *same environment* as beginner skiers, fear is something, however, which can and does affect ALL skiers.

The experienced skier will happily fly down the slope which would have a beginner skier fearing for their life and trembling in a sweaty mess. However, that very same experienced skier may go cold and their body stiffen at the mere thought of skiing across ice, or down really steep slopes, or on moguls (bumps).

Although everyone may differ in the cause of their own fear, everyone tends to experience fear in a very similar way.

In what situations do you experience fear when skiing?

All the time on every run? Some beginners often experience fear on every run. Is that you?

Perhaps you don't like going fast because you are afraid of being out-of-control and falling and hurting yourself?

For more advanced skiers, perhaps, you hate bumps and moguls? Though in reality, you avoid mogul runs because you are actually scared of them? Scared of falling. Scared of hurting yourself, or embarrassing yourself.

Do really steep slopes scare you?

Maybe you are afraid of going off-piste, whilst at the same time, envying those skiers you see blasting a trail through waist-deep powder snow.

All these fears and concerns are holding you back from improving your skiing. Whilst improving your skiing *DOES* require learning new technical skiing skills, sometimes, by far the biggest factor holding you back is purely mental.

What is NLP?

Neuro-linguistic programming, or NLP, is a cognitive technology founded upon multiple disciplines and organised by Richard Bandler and John Grinder. It dates back to the 1970's when Dr. Grinder was a professor of linguistics at the University of California in Santa Cruz, and Bandler was a student of mathematics and computers. Based upon their experiences with modelling various therapies with much success, they devised *a model of communication* that incorporated how people get *"programmed"* by linguistic and sensory influences to produce habitual and systematic behaviours.

What Bandler and Grinder invented was a modelling technology that provides new methods to exact change in individuals, and a means to model excellence which accelerates the speed of learning. In effect, "NLP offers a model for learning how to recognise excellence and how to emulate it".

In a step-by-step fashion, NLP provides a model that teaches us how to achieve excellence in any chosen subject.   Whether that subject is communication skills, building rapport, or even learning how to ski, NLP provides a model that can be used to build your skills and model excellence in any chosen discipline.

Does NLP work? Will it improve my skiing?

NLP does not need any preset or required beliefs, nor assumptions to work. It is a tool, not a religion.   There is no need to subscribe to the presuppositions of NLP for it to work. In fact, the only measure of an NLP model is whether it works or does not work.

In short, the best way to understand NLP and allow it to help you involves actually **experiencing** it. However, this book will only help you *improve your skiing* if you actually *do the exercises* within.

Let's do a quick, short exercise now, designed to allow you to experience NLP.

Don't just read it; please *do the exercise.*

Exercise : Introduction to NLP for Skiing

1.   Can you remember a specific time when you were skiing successfully on piste? If you've never skied before, I want you to *imagine that you can already ski,* and create a waking "dream" of false memories where you are skiing successfully.

2. Imagine you are watching yourself ski from a distance – Can you imagine being down at the bottom of the slope looking up, watching your own self skiing down that slope on that very occasion. Notice how you feel when you watch yourself skiing from this distant perspective. Be aware of how those images make you feel in your body.

3. Now, relive the actual experience.   Transport yourself back into your memory of that specific time. See your skis below you. Feel the chilly breeze on your face as you ski. Feel the snow passing under your skis. See the scenery changing as you ski down the slope. Hear the "schhhhhhhhh" sound of the skis sliding on the snow. Notice exactly how you feel as you re-experience the event, seeing the things you saw, hearing the sounds you heard then.

You will notice that your feelings during each of these two different visualisations are very distinct from each other. Being *in* the scene, being part of it, is a hugely different experience from watching yourself in the third person. Being in the scene is what NLP calls "*associated*", whereas watching yourself from the distant perspective is called "*disassociated*".

NOTE: If you didn't *do the exercise*, instead have merely read it, please go back immediately and actually *do the exercise*. This book will only help you *improve your skiing* when you actually *do the exercises* within. They are well worth taking time over as you will benefit *only* by experiencing them.

What we have learnt is: if you want to get excited about an experience, you need to get involved by stepping *into* the experience both physically and mentally. By stepping *out* of experiences, you disassociate from them. This effect can be very useful for dealing with unpleasant memories as it gives us techniques we can use to actually *alter* how you experience those memories.

By the end of the book, you will become much more resourceful – both being able to enhance your positive experiences and build upon them, and diminish, or even eliminate the effects of any negative experiences so you are no longer affected by them.

A little bit about how NLP works.

Aristotle wrote, *"Spoken words are the symbols of mental experience and written words are the symbols of spoken words. Just as all men have not the same writing, so all men have not the same speech sounds, but the mental experiences which these directly symbolise are the same for all, as also are those things of which our experiences are the images."*

Basically, Aristotle is saying that words symbolise our mental experiences. Our language not only reflects our experience, but filters and shapes it too. As the founders of NLP, Bandler and Grinder, point out: *"The nervous system which is responsible for producing the representational system of language is the same nervous system by which humans produce every other model of the world – visual, kinaesthetic, etc. The same principles of structure are operating in each of these systems."*

NLP thus uses linguistic and visualisation elements to alter exactly how our representations of events and memories are coded in our brains.

Let's look at what can hold you back from improving your skiing.

There are five fundamental aspects that can hold you back from improving your skiing.

❖ Lack of desire for improvement

❖ Lack of technical skill or knowledge

❖ Fear

❖ Lack of self-belief

❖ Over-confidence *(this is most often expressed by simply skiing out-of-control)*

It is my belief that you actively want and desire to overcome your fears and thus improve your skiing, and that you are *willing* to take the actions necessary to improve your skiing; such as reading this book thoroughly right through to the end.

A Note on Self-Sabotage

It may be that although you *appear* to desire to overcome your fears, you actually gain something from having them and keeping them. Perhaps, it means you gain more attention from loved ones. Perhaps it gives you a reason to reject skiing because you do not TRULY wish to learn to ski. Perhaps your fears allow you to define yourself and maintain a particular self-image – "Now I am a mother, I am more afraid of hurting myself".

Robert Dilt writes in "Beliefs": *"When you put your resources and energy into a goal that you're not congruent about, some part of you will fight the change and probably keep it from happening".*

In any of these cases, this book *simply will not be able to help.* In order to be able to produce effective results, you must *truly desire* to want to ski without fear. You must truly desire to overcome your fears and anxieties.

Even if you pick up just one little tool or technique from this book that can help, it will be worth the investment of your time.

If you lack technical skiing skills, then I suggest you book a private lesson or two with a great ski instructor. Look for an instructor that has lots of recommendations from people who were at a similar level of skiing ability as you.

To find a great instructor, ask around. Ask your chalet hosts. Ask at the local dry ski slope.

If you can possibly help it, my advice is not to bother with group lessons at ski school as progress is typically very slow in a group environment and the "follow-me-down-the-hill" technique still employed by many ski schools, especially in Europe, does not lend itself to *rapid, concentrated* learning, nor will it actively help you to overcome your fears! You will barely learn in six days, what you could learn in an hour or so with a decent private ski instructor.

Coming back to the fundament aspects that hold you back in skiing, the last three aspects (fear, lack of self-belief, and over-confidence) are all internal mental issues - which is the speciality subject where NLP excels.

NLP can give you tools and techniques to be able to change, or "hack", your previous mental programming to overcome fears, build your confidence, and reproduce your peak performance repeatedly – *whenever you choose.*

When you experience NLP, you will notice the direct connections between your mind, body and nervous systems. Please note that while **"NLP provides the methods and technology for the "how-to" of the managing of thoughts"**, it is for you to *implement* the techniques you learn, and to identify exactly *when* using these techniques in the field would best help you to improve your skiing. I will provide some guidance and suggest when different exercises can be useful.

Teaching your subconscious to ski

Whilst most of us are only really aware of our conscious mind on a day to day basis, it is, in fact, your *subconscious* mind that actually skis. Your subconscious mind may take **suggestions** from your conscious mind, *if it chooses.* Suggestions such as "turn left now to avoid that steep section", "bend your knees" or "lean forward".

However, have you ever had the experience where you have said to yourself, "Turn here... Turn now." and yet your body was simply frozen, unable to commence the turn? Your conscious mind is busy giving orders or instructions, however, once you fully realise that it is your subconscious mind that has full control of your body, so you will understand why you remained frozen, unable to commence the turn: your subconscious mind was ignoring the suggestion.

So it is, in fact, actually your subconscious mind that has the tough, and often underappreciated, job of skiing.

You might find that thought rather weird, however bear with me just a moment, and play with me just a little. I'd like to do a small demonstration.

Raise your right hand 10 centimetres and clench your fist. Go on, *do it*!
Play with me!
Now lower it again.

You should notice that you didn't actually have to think about WHICH muscles to use, nor in what order. It was your subconscious mind that actually produced the behaviour.

So it is with skiing.

It is your subconscious mind which needs to learn how to ski.

Your subconscious mind needs to learn how to adopt the correct stance. Your subconscious mind needs to learn how to use your leg and thigh muscles and upper body to keep your weight in the right position at the right time; to control your centre of gravity, to allow your skis to turn. Your subconscious mind needs to learn to *trust itself* to control something that is sliding on snow, and thus basically out-of-control.

All these muscle movements and belief processes are all processes which actually occur subconsciously.

You do, however, use your conscious mind to help your subconscious to learn all that. What is entirely conscious at first, becomes subconscious as you practise it.

Learning to ski is like any complex process you learn: there are a number of stages you go through with your learning.

1. Unconscious incompetence. This is the stage of someone who has never thought about learning to ski. You do not know that you don't know how to ski – simply because you have never ever thought about it.

2. Conscious Incompetence. This is the stage of the absolute beginner – you are aware that you do not know how to ski. You learn fast at this stage because the less that you know, the greater the opportunity for improvement.

3. Conscious Competence. This is where beginner is starting to get it. You are aware that you are learning and see a vast improvement over when you first started to ski. You still need to concentrate as your skill is not yet consistent and habitual. You still have to think about situations; finding the right line, you occasionally fall when bumps or ice take you unawares.

4. Unconscious Competence. You do not have to think about skiing. Your subconscious mind now does the skiing for you, and your conscious mind is free to do something else such as enjoying the view, planning the route, etc. Your skill is thus habitual and completely automatic.

5. Mastery. This is the expert – who can recover from situations where a lesser-experienced skier would fall, and they do it without even thinking or being aware of it! You fly down the mountain off-piste down the steepest slopes looking graceful and elegant. Everything seems to flow and even the moguls seem to help you. Watching you ski is beautiful as you make everything look easy.

In addition, people *do not* process language consciously either. We process language at the subconscious level. Words are merely anchors for experiences; *surface structures* which attempt to represent or express deeper and more conceptual structures. Sure, you may process the concepts *expressed by language* consciously, however that is all done in conjunction with your subconscious mind. After all, you do not have to stop to think about what each and every word means.

Sigmund Freud wrote: *"Words and magic were in the beginning one and the same thing, and even today words retain much of their magical power. By words, one of us can give another the greatest happiness or bring about utter despair; by words the teacher imparts his knowledge to the student; by words the orator sweeps his audience with him and determines its judgements and decisions. Words call forth emotions and are universally the means by which we influence our fellow-creatures."*

I have phrased various concepts throughout this book in a very specific way, designed to actually work *with* your subconscious – for example, various *hypnotic* commands. These were used most successfully by Milton Erickson, who was a leading practitioner of medical hypnosis. He realised that there are multiple levels of perception and response, not all of which are at the conscious level of awareness, but were at levels of understanding not recognised by the conscious self. I have tried to incorporate some of his methodology in this book: techniques such as *embedded commands*.

By reading this book, I assume that you therefore give me permission to use such 'hypnotic' techniques to help you to feel more confident when you are skiing. It is quite subtle, and for most people, you will not even be aware of when this technique is being used. For those people reading this who are sceptical of such methods, I hope you can *allow* me to indulge in this privilege of talking to your subconscious mind directly from time to time.

I would like to talk briefly about hypnosis as it is one of the most commonly misunderstood terms. When most people think about hypnosis, they think of stage shows for entertainment, hocus pocus, and people in strange sleep-like trances. However, most people actually experience a form of hypnotic trance on a daily basis: have you ever watched television? Have you ever experienced a book so entrancing that you have lost complete track of time because you were so absorbed in it?

Erickson writes, *"Anything that fascinates and holds or absorbs a person's attention could be described as hypnotic. We have the concept of the common everyday trance for those periods in everyday life when we are so absorbed or preoccupied with one matter or another that we momentarily lose track of our outer environment"*.

Please think of hypnosis in the context of NLP as a trance-like state where you have limited focus of attention that is directed inwards, inside yourself.

Did you actually *do the exercise* earlier? If so, great!

If not, you (your conscious mind) may have *chosen* to not do the exercise, but from now on, I wonder if you would give yourself the opportunity to experience the benefits of NLP fully. If you skipped the exercise, perhaps you notice that a part of yourself is *feeling incomplete or even slightly guilty* as a result; like you feel slightly that you are missing part of the bigger picture. So, I wonder if you would be willing to experience the benefits of NLP fully yet? If so, it is okay to turn back to the exercise and give it a go now. After all, this book can only help you to *improve your skiing* when you actually *do the exercises* contained within.

NLP Presuppositions – and how they apply to skiing.

There are a number of presuppositions – or assumptions – in NLP that are central principles; like a guiding philosophy. You do not need to believe that they are true or universal. However, they are very useful and powerful for helping us to create models of excellence which help us to achieve what we want more easily.

1. The map is not the territory. Everyone experiences the world differently. I have a different experience of reality than you do. However, what is important is that *people respond to their experience of reality,* not to reality itself. Unfortunately, our beliefs do not always reflect reality accurately, neither are they etched in stone; instead they are merely written on our map of reality. Consequently, we must ask ourselves whether our current 'map' is the most useful. In the skiing context: the expert skier looks at the same slope in a very different way from the beginner. As a more experienced skier, if you ski a run you were scared by when you were a beginner, you'll now experience it in a very different way.

2. Experience has a structure. Our whole experience of reality is based entirely on information that comes from our five senses: visual, auditory, kinaesthetic (touch), olfactory (smell) or gustatory (taste). We compare our sensory experience with our accumulated history and thus create meaning or reality for ourselves. The human brain has a tendency to use shortcuts on meaning – we tend to make use of what has worked for us before. We have patterns or habitual responses that we use as shortcuts to enable us to respond to different situations quicker. However, this also means that each of us can create different meanings from the same set of sensory data.

These shortcuts can create problems with fear on the slopes – where your subconscious mind automatically produces a fear response which is out of context with the actual risk!

3. If one person can do something, anyone can learn to do it. When you see other skiers flying down the slope, know that their talent is simply a set of internal resources – beliefs, emotions, motor-movements and balance - that have been combined, sequenced and practised until they have become an automatic skill. To be a fantastic skier like them, you need to simply learn their exact strategies for producing that behaviour, and reproduce them yourself.

In fact, until the 1950's people thought that skiing was simply a matter of talent, rather than skill. But black and white films were made of successful skiers and researchers then studied these frame by frame, and broke the skiers' movements down into the smallest possible units of behaviour. When beginners were taught these same movements, their ability to learn to ski improved dramatically.

4. The mind and body are parts of the same system. If you want to feel depressed, hunch your shoulders, drop your chin, look towards the ground, breathe shallow. Very shortly you will start to feel more depressed. If you want to feel confident and capable, puff your chest out, breathe deeply, smile at yourself, raise your chin and look up. Thus, our minds and thoughts constantly affect our emotions, just as our bodies affect our emotions and thoughts.

5. People already have all the resources they need to make any desired change. You may however have to learn how to apply them in the appropriate context.

6. You cannot NOT communicate. Even by yourself, your inner voice is rarely silent for long. Also, other non-verbal communication such as your body language and posture speaks volumes about how you view yourself. Your inner voice can either support you in your learning to ski, or it can hinder you. We deal with how to manage your inner voice in a later chapter.

7. The meaning of your communication is the response you elicit. There are no failures in communication: only response and result. Your inner voice can talk you into being afraid to ski, afraid of falling, or afraid of going too fast. What you give awareness to in your mind affects your emotional state. Unfortunately, the fearful person then fully associates into their internal representation of danger, thus disempowering themselves from their full resources.

8. Underlying every behaviour is a positive intention. From fear of falling to that self-critical voice in your head telling you that you'll never learn to ski, every single behaviour has a positive intention. It is designed to protect you from harm; be that emotional or physical danger. Even expressing criticism can reflect a subconscious desire to be acknowledged.

9. People are always making the best choices available to them. Everyone's map of reality is different. Consequently, people make what we think are poor choices not because they want to, but because they do not perceive any better options or choice available to them. Based on prior experience, *unconsciously* those are the best choices available to them.

10. If what you are doing isn't working, do something else. Do anything else. If you always do what you've always done, you'll always get what you've always got. If that is not delivering the goods, then change it. If you are constantly falling over skiing, then something in the way you are using your body and mind, is directly responsible for it. Change it and see if it improves your skiing!

11. There is no failure, only feedback. Falling over once is not a failure to learn to ski. You would have to be pretty hard on yourself to believe that. However, neither is falling over 10 times, or a hundred times nor a thousand. My personal belief is that if "you don't fall over, you're not trying hard enough".

NLP is about changing your internal representations

The basic tenet of NLP is that you can change your feelings by changing *how* you *internally represent* an experience.

Can you remember a specific memory of skiing which has left you with unpleasant memories or emotions?

Reducing Fear Caused by a Specific Event Whilst Skiing

The following exercise is designed to allow you to reduce fears and anxieties that were caused by a specific non-traumatic event that occurred to you whilst skiing. It gives you an example of how you can change your own internal representation of events and thus also actually change your feelings towards that experience. To eliminate fears caused by serious traumatic events, see the exercise on eliminating fears caused by previous injuries in the following chapter.

Exercise: Eliminating Negative Emotions with Incongruent Ski Movie Music

1. Watch movie of your unpleasant skiing memory. Begin by thinking of a specific memory that occurred *whilst you were skiing* that has left you with unpleasant memories or emotions. For example, recall a time when you fell badly, or when you were out of control, or just plain embarrassed. Choose a specific and real event from your past. When you think of this event, make a mental note of what images and sounds you remember and watch a mental movie of this event occurring before you. Once the movie ends, notice carefully how you are feeling.

2. Select incongruent music. Now, think of some theme music that gives you the *complete opposite* of the feelings you got from your mental movie. Choose something completely disparate. For example, if my movie is of me out of control, I like to choose the *theme from Ski Sunday* (a British tv ski programme), or if my movie is of a time when I was particularly scared whilst skiing, I'd choose *Come Fly with Me,* others might choose *Ride of the Valkyries* or perhaps the *James Bond* theme music, or the theme from the *Muppets* .

3. Repeat your mental movie with the music. Now you have chosen contrasting theme music, re-run your "ski" movie in your head *a couple of times.* Each time, play your selected incongruent music nice and loud in your head. Continue the music right through to the end of your mental movie.

4.   Check your results. Rewind the movie in your head back to the beginning – and re-play it, but this time without the music. Notice the results. Have your feelings changed? For a lot of people, the event has become humorous or absurd, unpleasant feelings diminished or lost. If you are not yet satisfied by the results, try re-selecting different types of theme music to find one that works for you.

Successfully completing this exercise provides a demonstration of the NLP supposition that **Experience has a structure**. Before the exercise, your structure of the memory contained a serious emotional event with unpleasant feelings. After running the exercise successfully, your actual memory of it was fundamentally changed by the addition of the incongruent music to such an extent that your base feelings about the memory were altered too.

If you have successfully completed the exercise, you'll notice that it no longer affects you like it did.

Will the change last?

You are fully capable of undoing this positive effect by re-running the movie in your head without the incongruent music. Also, if you associate into the negative memory, then you are capable of undoing the effect.

Eliminating Your Fears

"Your feelings come from how you think about people, events, circumstances, or things, not the people, events, circumstances, and things themselves!" – Andreas & Faulkner from "NLP, the New Technology of Achievement".

Everyone has fears that can be out of proportion with the actual danger faced in some situations. The problem rises though when our ability to perform well is impaired by such an out-of-proportion fear. As such, fear is direct communication from your subconscious mind. Your subconscious is trying to let you know that you need to be careful as danger is present.

True Fear and Faux-Fear

There are actually *two* different types of fear:

One type of fear acts to heighten our perception, releases adrenaline, increases our breathing, increases our heartbeat, and our pupils dilate to heighten our visual perception. All ready for a "fight-or-flight" response.

29

Thus, it acts to increase our abilities to perform beyond our normal capabilities. This type of fear is produced when there is an actual risk and is a *healthy response* to an actual danger. It is our body's natural response to danger and challenge.

This type of fear is our physiological reaction designed to protect you, to prevent you from risk of injury and risk to life and limb. We do not want to mess with true fear as it serves you well; it helps to prevent injury and death.

The other type of fear, faux-fear, distorts our perceptions, immobilises us, and decreases our ability to ski well. It exaggerates the risk of falling to a broken leg; it steepens the slope ahead of you to a near cliff, and reduces how you perceive your own skiing abilities. In other words, it amplifies the significance of the danger.

This type of fear is created when there is a *perceived* risk. Our body's response is to stiffen, to lose flexibility, and we have a tendency to stop breathing. It is an illusion though – which results in diminished self-image, under-achieving, and can be self-perpetuating. By skiing stiffly and without flexibility, we are actually more prone to falling. A negative self-image will then feed upon an actual reduced performance, and increase anxiety for future ski runs.

I shall call this second type of fear faux-fear, meaning false fear, as it is not based upon reality, but upon a *distorted interpretation* of reality. Think of it as an acronym for "*False Evidence Appearing Real*". It takes unsupported notions of impending doom, amplifies them, and then presents the anticipated results as inevitable failure.

To produce faux-fear, you need to experience the *threat of risk* – that something is capable of doing you harm; either to your body or to your ego. You need a *sense of vulnerability* – that it is able to harm you. It also needs a *lack of confidence* in your ability to overcome the danger.

The fearful person associates into their internal representation of danger. They increase their perception (known as submodalities in NLP terminology) of the experience such as the size, closeness, and steepness of the slope so that the threat appears greater than their resources. They diminish submodalities of their own resources, such as their memories of success. They may activate another set of beliefs that involves the estimate of the importance of what others may think of them.

Synaesthesia is a phenomenon where a sensation that normally occurs in one sense modality occurs when another modality is stimulated; where one sense leads to an automatic, involuntary experience in a second sense. We all experience synaesthesia: Pictures that evoke feelings, music or sounds that evoke shapes and colours. For example, when you merely see someone scraping their nails down a blackboard, it may well induce that sound in your mind and set your teeth on edge.

When we are fearful and anxious though, synaesthesia happens more frequently and with less conscious awareness. This can lead to the belief that your feelings of fear "*just happen*", or that they are actually caused *by* the environment, rather than being a result of your *attention* to your representation of "danger".

Note: You can experience both types of fear at the same moment. Skiing at an advanced level on seriously steep slopes is a prime example of an activity where you can experience both types of fear simultaneously.

The Three Main Fears in Skiing

There are three main fears in skiing. These are:

Fear of Falling

- What if I fall and hurt myself.

- I don't want to injure my knee again.

- I am really cold and wet from falling over so much on this snow.

- I don't like being out of control – sliding is out of control.

- What if I can't stop, get faster and faster and crash. I'll definitely break something.

Fear of Failing

- Everyone else is doing really well. I don't want to be the slowest in the group.

- It will be so humiliating if I fall. I'll be the only one who has fallen on this slope.

- If I fall now, everyone will see and laugh.

- Everyone is watching, so my reputation is at stake.

Fear of Flying *

* Thus named in the excellent book, "Inner Skiing" by Timothy Gallwey and Robert Kriegel.

- If I ski really well, everyone will think I am showing off.

Although your subconscious may recognise a particular situation almost instantly and produce its automated response, fear, without you having to consciously think about the imminent danger, a principle factor to remember is that your thoughts *do* actually precede your emotions and feelings.

Being afraid or feeling fear is a state. As such, your body has a strategy for how to produce and *maintain it*. The fear does not just happen. Your body reacts to an *external stimulus* with an *internal response* – but along the way, your mind creates meaning. Fear is not the direct response to the external stimulus: The ski slope simply is. The fear you feel is, in fact, your *response to the meaning that you attribute to the slope*. Your fear is a response to what you think skiing that slope *means to you*, what you think the outcome will be. After all, if you were 100% confident that you would

32

be able to ski the slope looking confident and stylish, how and why could you possibly be afraid of it?

Instead, you are afraid of what you *think* the 'probable outcome' will be when you ski it. Perhaps you are visualising falling (visual construction) or being hurt (kinaesthetic). Perhaps you are hearing laughing noises in your head from 'everyone' or your inner voice being critical (auditory construction) if you fall over. Perhaps the meaning you apply to falling over is that it confirms that 'you are useless at all sports' – thus you are afraid of falling as it would be confirmation of that belief system you have created.

Richard Bandler writes in "Time for a Change", "*People in the military learn to walk across a board. They walk across a board an inch off the floor. Put it up 20 feet. They move slower than they do on the ground. They look at the ground, taking in data they don't need. They only need data about the board. If they did it in the same way that they did on the ground, they could have the same result. By being **over** aware of height, they become **over** aware of the possibility of falling.*"

The next time you are on the ski slope, I want you to play really close attention to what you are doing with your mind in order to create that fear. I want you to be proud of your fear – after all, it is trying to *protect you* at some level. Being proud of your fear also gives you some control over it. When you feel the fear, what exactly are you aware of? What are you focussing on? How *do* you know that you feel fear? You might find that in order for you to feel fear you have to tense your muscles and breathe shallow and visualise falling. In which case, what happens when you consciously relax your muscles and breathe deeply? Does it help reduce the fearful emotion? We'll deal with negative visualisations shortly.

Misinterpretation of Fear

In Bandler and Grinders book, Frogs into Princes, they write:

"*One of the ways people really get into trouble is that they play psychiatrist with their own parts without being qualified. They interpret the messages they get from their own parts. So they begin to feel something and they name it "fear," when it may be some form of excitement, or some kind of aliveness, or anything. By naming it and then acting as if that is the case, they misinterpret their own internal communication as easily as they misinterpret communication externally".*

Here in Chamonix, the guests who stay at our chalet often experience a misinterpretation of fear when we take them up the Aiguille du Midi cable car – up to 3,842 metres. At that altitude, the air is actually much thinner than at sea level: Oxygen concentrations are approximately 60% of those at sea level. As a result, for most people, their heart rate must naturally increase to pump the same amount of oxygen around their body to their cells. The problem arises when they subconsciously misattribute this autonomous rise in heartbeat as a fearful response. This lack of oxygen also can cause light-headedness or dizziness, fatigue or weakness, nausea, shortness of breath – which can all be symptoms of fear. Thus, many people subconsciously sense the rise in heartbeat and need to attribute a cause to it – the most obvious being a response based upon fear – which they then attribute to the height.

If you enjoy horror movies, then you'll believe that fear can actually be exciting. Bizarrely, many people actually enjoy being afraid: enjoying the arousal that comes with the fight-or-flight response. Likewise in extreme skiing, part of the enjoyment of skiing the line comes from the fear itself, and the arousal it causes.

How Fears Affect Different Levels of Skier

Fear in Absolute Beginners:

If you have *never skied before* but are already experiencing fear, then this is because your subconscious is applying prior patterns of behaviour to an anticipated experience. In other words, you are projecting previous negative experiences onto something which you have never tried – effectively, you are building a fear of a sport which you have *never experienced before*. This projected fear is actually called anxiety. Anxiety is fear over a future event.

Typically, the way you create fear prior to learning is to create a series of visual images, and/or movies, which involve you being out of control, falling over and hurting yourself, or being laughed at; mental images where you make a fool of yourself or be ridiculed. Perhaps your inner voice is telling you that you will never live up to your own desires and expectations? Perhaps you are afraid you won't be any good at skiing?

The fearful absolute beginner focuses on what *could* go wrong. They build a very strong negative image, making it bright, loud and clear. Thus, they are immediately failing to give themselves a strong mental foundation for actually experiencing the sport.

In simple terms, you can make constructed images or talk yourself into feeling fear. There are lots and lots of ways of doing it.

By virtue of being a beginner, because the sheer number of possible constructed images far exceeds the number of positive previous skiing events you've actually experienced, it is very possible to grow your fears exponentially and at an alarming rate.

The unfortunate thing is that every actual experience of skiing after that is filtered and experienced *relative* to your previously created negative images: When you do fall over (as *everyone* does), it just serves to fulfil your prophesy, or to prove your negative inner voice right.

For most fearful skiers, their primary fear is a fear of falling and injuring themselves. If you suffer from a fear of failing – being unable to learn, or not progressing fast enough, or being afraid of humiliation – then these fears stem primarily from having an uncontrolled inner voice. We deal with how to get control of your inner voice and get it to support you in the chapter, "Building your confidence".

The following exercise is designed for beginners who are starting out who have a fear of falling. You can practise the visualisation aspects at home, and then use the exercise on the slopes whenever you feel any anxiety or fear of falling.

Exercise: Overcoming the Fear of Falling in Beginners

Firstly, please accept the fact that as a beginner you will fall over. No one in the history of skiing has ever learnt to ski without falling. Consequently, you *must* accept that falling is a part of the learning process – of course, you want to minimise the number of falls, but the problem comes when you are overly afraid of falling – and thus paralysed from actually learning by the fear of falling.

There are many ways that you can create your fear of falling. Perhaps you imagine the pain or humiliation of falling – in other words, you are creating kinaesthetic projections. Perhaps you visualise yourself falling. This is the "strategy" you use to create your fear.

These strategies can be so automatic and rapid that you are unaware of them – and experience merely the symptoms of fear. However, if you can become aware of which strategies you use to create your fears, then this gives you much more control over them.

Notes:

If you have fear due to previous injuries and are scared of hurting yourself, you should do the exercise on eliminating fears due to previous injuries on page 53 prior to this exercise.

As this is an exercise that is best performed actually on the ski piste, it is vital that you are learning on a slope that is appropriate to your level: that you are on the nursery slopes or beginners area. Also, I cannot stress enough how, especially in the early stages, one-on-one instruction from a good private instructor will help you to make the most rapid improvement to your skiing, and help you overcome your primary fears.

1. Stop and breath. Get your breathing under control. Do not over-respire, but gently wait and normalise your breathing. Do not hurry this process – and take all the time you need to get your breathing back to normal.

2. Relax your muscles. You will probably find that you have tensed all your muscles. Consciously, relax. You are not skiing right now. You are merely standing on a ski slope – so relax. Keep breathing normally. Be aware of any tight muscles and relax them.

3. Look up and look around. Look at the scenery, the mountains, the valley. Relax and enjoy the view, taking it all in. Look all around you and simply absorb your environment.

4. Visualisation from the third-person perspective. Can you visualise yourself from a third-person perspective? I want you to imagine that you are watching yourself skiing. Visualise yourself from below, pushing off gently, and skiing just a few short metres to come to a controlled stop just slightly further down the slope without falling. Do not visualise skiing the entire slope just yet: just a short section. Repeat this visualisation 4-5 times.

Be aware of how you feel in your body. Have you tensed back up? If so, consciously relax again. Keep your breathing normal and repeat the visualisation until you can do it without tensing your body or increasing your breathing.

5. Visualisation from the first-person perspective. Now, I want you to visualise yourself skiing exactly the same section, but this time, you should visualise it from the point of view of what you would see if you were actually skiing the section. Imagine how it will feel with the snow passing under your skis. Imagine how the view will change as you descend slowly under control. Imagine the sounds that the skis will make as you ski the slope. Imagine how it feels to ski under control and come to a controlled stop.

Again, be aware of how it feels in your body, and whether your breathing has changed. If so, get your breathing back to normal, un-tense those muscles, and repeat the visualisation until you can complete it without tensing your muscles or altering your breathing.

6. Check the results. Now you are about to ski the slope, how do you feel? Has the fear reduced? Again, check the tension in your muscles, check your breathing rate. On a scale of 1 to 10, where would you rate your fear? If it is any more than a 3, then repeat the visualisations. *Always visualise yourself skiing competently and completing the run standing up.*

Note: If you do fall ALL the time, then there is something fundamentally wrong with your technique or the slope is too steep for you. If the latter, move to a less steep slope or take a less direct route down the slope. If the former, then get a lesson. There is no physical reason why you cannot learn to ski.

Whilst this book is not about giving technical advice on how to ski, here is some simple advice: keep your weight forward. Beginners always have a tendency to lean back once they feel they are out of control which simply accelerates them down the slope and thus further out of control. Instead, consciously bring your weight forward and *down the slope* whenever you feel yourself getting out of control. I know this may seem counter-intuitive to most beginners, but bringing your weight forward pressurises the front of your skis which improves control. Stay calm and do not panic. If you find yourself going too fast, head sideways, rather than straight down the slope. You can thus use the lesser angle to slow you down and keep yourself under control. If you are afraid, then it is especially important not to let yourself get out of control or let it get too fast for you to handle.

Another tip is to not let your arms drop. Most people fall when they let their arms drop to their sides. Basically, imagine a tightrope walker, they hold their arms out for balance – so it is with skiing (although you should not have your arms out like a tightrope walker). Remember that a nice 'wide' stance is the most stable. If you find yourself getting out of balance, then consciously bring your arms up parallel to give yourself the most stable position.

Fear in Beginners

(green to blue run skiers)

What a lot of beginners fear is being out-of-control. They build up the perceived risk of falling in their minds – which makes their body tense, and awkward – this affects their dynamicism, flexibility and posture – and thus they actually become *more* prone to falling as a result. Or they ski the slope in an awkward manner not flowing down the piste, but backing away from it.

Lots of beginners are fearful of "ice" and icy conditions. I would like to make a small distinction here as most beginners actually mistakenly call "hard-packed snow" by this misnomer. Real "boilerplate" ice actually has a very different feel to it: rock-solid, smooth to the touch, near impossible to ski well – the best strategy for beginners and solid ice is to hold your stable posture until you have passed over it and onto some snow on the other side.

With hard-packed snow, having good sharp edges on your skis really helps. Keep your stable posture, and remember to keep your weight forward to pressurise the insides of the skis. This will help give you control on the hard-packed snow.

Remember that you do not have to take the direct line down the slope, nor ski the entire slope in one go. Use wide sweeping turns to control your speed, and turn slightly back up hill to keep your speed under control. Go slowly or stop when you feel yourself getting out of control or when the fear level rises. Also, remember that you should let your skis do the work. As you accelerate when you turn past the point where you are heading straight down the slope, remember to complete the turn and use the slope itself to slow yourself – turn slightly up hill to control your speed. Concentrate on keeping your balance, using your edges to control your turn. Keep breathing as you ski, and consciously un-tense any muscles that may have tightened up due to your fears and adrenaline.

Remember to keep your weight forward whilst you are in the turn to pressurise the front edges of your skis. This will help you stay controlled and to turn. If you start to get out of control, bring your arms up in front of you and keep your weight forward to keep stable and balanced, and turn up hill to kill your speed and regain control.

Fear in Intermediate Skiers

(confident red to black run skiers, or double black diamond in the US)

For some skiers, there is an interaction here between the desire to be able to ski steep black runs – self-image and ego - and the distance between their *actual* technical ability and *perceived* technical ability. In a group environment, this can lead to bowing to peer-pressure, and following the leader of the group down slopes for which the skier is not sure they are 100% ready yet.

The intermediate skier may try to ski the black run before they have conscious awareness that they are technically capable of skiing it. This manifests itself in fear when you are halfway down, past the easy section, when you arrive at the top of the crux of the piste looking down from the top of a slope far steeper than anything you have ever skied before. Chuck in some ice or moguls for good measure, and your confidence in your ability to cope with the situation dwindles. Even a competent red run skier can feel extremely out of their depth very quickly.

However, in this situation, most fearful skiers *can* actually ski the black steep slope BETTER than they imagine they can – if only they weren't so fearful. Again, think about skiing short sections of the slope, rather than the entire thing in one go. Ski from point to point under control until you have descended the entire slope. Stop and rest a few moments if you are getting tired, and keep your breathing under control. Consciously relax your muscles if you are tensing them.

Fearful skiers paralyse themselves by *concentrating* on their fears; fears of going out of control, fears of falling and fears of injury. Instead, you should concentrate on your current ability, skiing achievements, and successful past experiences. You should also be consciously analysing the slope to determine where you are going to turn; planning your route.

Visualise yourself skiing each section individually, rather than the entire slope. Visualise it from the point of view of what you would see if you were actually skiing the section. Imagine how it will feel with the snow passing under your skis. Imagine how the view will change as you descend slowly under control. Imagine the sounds that the skis will make as you ski the slope. Imagine where exactly you will turn. Try to imagine how the snow will be through your descent? Hard-pack or icy? If so, imagine how you will edge your skis to keep control, how you will keep your balance down the slope.

Be aware of any tension in your muscles – and repeat the visualisation exercise 4-5 times until you are able to do it without increasing your breathing or tensing your muscles. Check your fear level – if it is above a 3, continue with the visualisation exercises.

When you come to ski the slope, remember to relax your muscles and keep breathing as you ski.

Note that, at this level on steep icy slopes, the fear of injury may be an actual risk, as well as a perceived risk if you let yourself get out of control.

Fear in Advanced Skiers

(Beyond black runs: off-piste, moguls, steeps).

At the higher levels of the sport, the actual risks are elevated, and advanced skiers, through their past ski experiences, normally have a much better mental conditioning and a better toolset with dealing with *perceived* risk. They have a strong self-belief in their abilities as a skier, albeit perhaps in certain specific situations.

A lot of skiers hold themselves back from learning how to ski off-piste. They might hold the belief that off-piste skiing is inherently dangerous or avalanche-prone. They might have a go, fall over a few times, and thus be reminded of all the falls and their experience of learning how to ski as a beginner, and then decide that they '*prefer*' skiing on-piste.

A lot of skiers shy away from moguls: primarily because they haven't learnt the technique to ski moguls well. To learn the technical ability, a day with a great ski instructor will probably work wonders here. My ability on moguls improved and my fears reduced when I spent the whole day looking for moguls and skiing them with a friend who *LOVES* moguls.

The steeper the slope, the greater the fear. Steep slopes can create fear for the simple reason that the risk of actual danger *is* elevated. However NLP techniques can be useful to keep faux-fear under control, whilst you appreciate the real dangers of steep slopes.

If you are an advanced skier, you have probably already learned how to control your fears to a certain extent, though there may be specific situations where you still feel afraid. Some of the exercises around building confidence may still be useful, likewise some of the exercises in the chapter on achieving peak performance – specifically anchoring your most resourceful state for skiing so you can get into that state whenever you wish.

Exercises for common fearful situations.

Eliminating Doubts in Your Ability to Learn to Ski

This next exercise will help you change your internal representation of your fear of learning to ski. It should help build your confidence in your ability to learn to ski, whilst removing any doubts in your ability to learn the sport.

You can use it at home or on the slopes – though it is better if you practise it at home first. Find a quiet place where you will not be disturbed, breathe deeply and relax for a moment or two.

Exercise: Improving Your Confidence in Your Ability to Learn to Ski

1. Think of a belief you know is true. I want you to stop and think of something you absolutely believe 100%. Just stop. Think about it. Think about something you know. Is the sun coming up tomorrow? Is breathing useful?

I want to you to notice *where* the voice comes from that confirms this.

42

Does it come from ahead? In front of you? From the left or right side? Up or down? Kind of all over? What we are doing here is identifying how you represent beliefs to yourself: in NLP terms, we are identifying the submodalities necessary for it to be a belief.

2.   Think of something that may or may not be true? Think of something you are not sure about. What do you want for lunch? White cars are driven by safer drivers than silver cars. The health and education systems are improving as a result of government reforms. By 2020, 95% of the world will have broadband internet access.

Again, notice *where* that voice comes from. *Where* are the pictures located in your mind?

Here, we are identifying how you represent doubts to yourself: identifying the submodalities necessary for it to be a doubt.

We have now identified a strong belief and a doubt. In most people, the strong belief is located straight ahead, and the doubt is located to the left, lower.

Is one bigger or smaller? Normally the strong belief is bigger.

3. Are you afraid to ski? If your response is from straight ahead, I want you to actively move the fear. Move the voice down to the left where your doubting beliefs were located, move the pictures down to the left. Make the voice or images smaller, quieter. Shrink the image, mute the voice. Make the image dark and fuzzy and difficult to see. And very very small.

4. I am learning to be a *great* skier. Take that thought and the images it gives you. Take the voice. Now move it straight ahead in front of you. Up close and personal. Make it big, bright and loud. I am learning to be a *great* skier. What happens if you change the tone of the voice? For some people, deepening the tone of the voice to a lower tone helps increase the intensity of the belief. Close your eyes. Now, double the size of the picture. Quadruple the volume of the voice. Turn up the brightness even more. Increase the volume yet more.

5. Now look at your skis – or visualise them straight ahead if they are not at hand. Repeat the last step again – I am learning to be a *great* skier - five times *really quickly* whilst looking at your skis. This time, when you turn the dial up on the volume of the voice, forget turning it up to eleven – turn it up to twenty-seven! I am learning to be a *great* skier. Make your visual images enormous.

Whenever you have any doubts in your ability to learn, repeat this exercise a few times.

Eliminating Negative Anchors Attached to Skiing

Any time you are in an *intense* emotional state, you are susceptible to creating anchors. Anything specific that happens around you can get instantly connected with the way that you feel at that moment. Thereafter, each and every time you repeat or trigger that anchor, you get the same emotional response.

For example, perhaps you can think of a song that you love which instantly makes you feel good whenever you hear it. It will affect your heart rate, your breathing; perhaps even create goose-bumps. You could be feeling down, but when that song comes on the radio, you instantly feel better. This is all automatic and subconscious. That is what we call an 'anchor'.

Just as anchors can be created to positive experiences, they can be created to negative experiences too.

Imagine if you feel a lot of fear the first time you ever go skiing. It would be possible that the strong emotion of fear could become anchored to the mere sight of skis, or a chair lift if you fell off awkwardly when you first tried to get off one.

If you have these negative anchors, it means that until you experience *a strong positive emotion* in the company of skis or a chair lift, etc., you will *always* trigger that fearful emotion every time you see a pair of skis or a chair lift.

If you find that you have a spontaneously negative state, then most probably you have a negative anchor which is creating this response.

Exercise: Collapsing Negative Anchors Attached to Skiing.

1. Identify the negative anchor. Firstly, you need to identify the specific negative anchor. You need to work out what *specifically* is causing you to first have a negative response. Is it the sight of skis? Is it the sight of the slopes or a sign? Once, you have identified the exact anchor, we can use NLP to collapse the negative associations you experience with that anchor.

This is the hardest part of this exercise as anchors work unconsciously, bypassing conscious thought.   Think back until you come to the moment when your mood was positive and you felt fine. As you play your memory back, ask yourself, "what was my mood at this specific moment in time?" Now, come forward again, until you discover the specific moments when your mood changed. The trigger for the negative anchor is located in that moment in time. Once you recall a change in your mood, try to pin down what exactly was happening. Where were you exactly? What were you looking at? What did you hear? What were you thinking about?

2. Break your negative state. Briefly think about a favourite piece of music or tv programme. Think about what you ate for breakfast.

3. Recall a positive state. Can you remember a time when you felt 100% confident and 100% happy. Recall all the positive emotions. Breath like you were breathing then. Stand like you were standing. Bring all the happy memories flooding back – relive the experience fully in your mind. If you can, amplify it even more to make the positive experience even more positive. Make all the sounds brighter and louder. Make all the colours even more vivid and in high definition. Really feel the emotion you felt at that time.

4. Now, create a positive anchor. Whilst you are re-experiencing all this positive emotion, *when you are at the peak of the positive emotion*, tap yourself with an open hand quite strongly on the chest twice. This will create a positive anchor: you should experience those positive emotions the next time you tap yourself in the same manner.

5. Trigger both anchors at the same time. Because you have identified your negative anchor, you can deliberately set it off. What you must do, is simultaneously set off your positive anchor at the same time – tap yourself with your open hand twice on the chest – just immediately after you see/set off the negative anchor.

If now, when you experience your negative anchor you are unable to easily experience the unresourceful or negative state, then you have successfully collapsed your negative anchor.

Troubleshooting:
Cause: If the unpleasant feelings were not neutralised, were your positive experiences strong enough to neutralise the negative ones? You need a positive anchor *at least* of the same strength as the power of the negative anchor.

Solution: Re-run the exercise, but really amplify the positive experiences. You can layer the positive experiences from several memories with the same positive anchor to increase the power and potency of the positive emotion. This is called "Stacking states". The most important thing is that the positive state that you trigger must be stronger than the negative state in order to collapse the anchor.

Sometimes the power of the negative anchor is such that it is next to impossible to go from a negative state to a positive one directly in one step. What you can do is create a *series* of different positive anchors and fire these off slowly one after the other as your state transforms. Thus, you progressively change your state from a negative one to a positive one. Eg. Negative state -> slightly negative -> neutral -> slightly positive -> positive.

Creating Different Anchors for Different Positive Empowering Emotions

You can create different positive anchors for different emotions. For example, you could create an anchor which brings you strong feelings of confidence. Simply bring back those memories of a specific time when you felt fully 100% confident, and create a specific anchor for that.

You could also create an anchor, for example, of a time when you felt particularly courageous.

Once you have several different anchors for different positive and empowering emotions, what you can do is layer those anchors. The next time you are faced with a slope that would daunt you, you can fire off both of those anchors one after the other to simultaneously to bring back both your feelings of confidence and courageousness. This will put you in the most resourceful state for skiing the slope.

I find I ski best when I am both relaxed, clear of mind, and slightly aggressive – consequently I have created an anchor which puts me in this state whenever I trigger it. Thus, I am able to access my most resourceful state for skiing whenever I wish.

Just remember to use a unique and specific anchor for each different emotion. You can create anchors using a specific touch, or even a particular phrase toned in a unique way. The important thing to remember is that the anchor should be unique.

There is more on building and using anchors in the chapter, "Achieving Peak Performance".

Eliminating Negative Emotion Attached to Specific Memories of Bad Experiences.

The following exercise is a great tool to use when you have a *specific* memory of a bad experience while skiing, or learning to ski. You can use it either at home to eliminate the emotional content of your bad memories, or on the slope when you are affected by it.

Exercise: Eliminate Negative Emotions by Running a Movie Backwards

1. Think of an unpleasant memory. Think of a specific time when you fell over skiing when it badly affected your confidence or where you were hurt by it, and run a movie of it in your head, however you remember it now. Notice whatever negative, unpleasant or fearful feelings you have. Play the movie all the way through to the end.

2. Run the same movie backwards. Start from the very end of that movie, but this time, run the entire movie backwards in rewind mode, in full technicolour, and *extremely fast*, so that it only takes about one and a half *seconds* to rewind. Just as if time itself were running backwards at warp speed. Once you are back at the beginning, jump straight to the very end of the movie again without playing it forwards in your head, and re-run this backwards movie *extremely quickly* 5 - 10 times more.

3. Test your experience. Now, re-run the same movie forwards again, and be aware of how your feelings have changed as a response to the exercise.

If you are like most people, you will find that your original unpleasant feelings associated with the event have been negated. By running it backwards at speed like this, it is like your experience of the event has been so scrambled that it is impossible to feel the fear or negative emotion when you re-run your memory of the event again.

Troubleshooting:
Cause: If the unpleasant feelings were not neutralised, were you actually IN the movie, experiencing it, getting the sensations of moving backward? More likely you were watching a movie of yourself playing backwards from a third-person perspective – watching yourself in the movie - rather actually reliving the event backwards itself.

Solution: Re-run the exercise, but when you come to run the movie in fast-rewind this time, fully associate into the memory, and imagine you are actually catapulted back through the experience by an enormous springboard or elastic band in time; sucked back in time by a giant vacuum cleaner.

Note: sometimes running this exercise whilst disassociated from the movie can benefit. Rather than being IN the movie, run it as if you were watching yourself in it – change the movie to black and white and make the movie screen small whilst running it forwards. Then flip it into colour when you play it in super-fast rewind mode.

For really traumatic events – if you have no fear of heights, you could watch your movie of the same experience from an aerial perspective from 50 metres up above the event. Then, just at the very moment the scene ends, fall from your aerial perspective right into the end of the scene just as you hit super-fast rewind, and imagine yourself being sucked back through the entire experience in one and half seconds.

This exercise is fantastic for eliminating strong unpleasant feelings in memories that can still affect you.

Reducing Anxiety Over a Specific Event or Ski Piste

The following exercise is great for skiers of all levels to reduce the amount of anxiety they may be feeling over a specific event or experience, such as a specific ski piste. It can be used at home or on the slopes. In either location, you can relax and breathe easily. Let all the muscles in your body relax....

Exercise: "Timeline" Technique to Reduce Anxiety for a Specific Event

1. Find your time line. I want you to imagine an enormous filing cabinet. Inside that filing cabinet are thousands upon thousands of folders. Each folder is filled with a single memory of every event which you have ever experienced, or ever will experience in the future. These folders are filed in time-order sequentially, and hence contain your entire experience of life dating back from your very first memory right through to the moment you die.

2. Float above your timeline. Float above the folders and go out into the future – one minute after the *successful completion* of the ski run which you are anxious about. Open the folder containing the memory of completing the ski run successfully. Play the memory it contains. Fully associate into the memory it contains... Make the images bright and the colours vivid. Make the sounds loud.

3. Look back towards now. Now, where's the anxiety?

4. Put the folder back and close the cabinet.

Troubleshooting

If you don't get reduced feelings of anxiety, it might mean one of the following common problems:

Cause: You have not *fully associated* into seeing the successful completion of the ski piste

Solution: Re-run the exercise and make sure your visual image of skiing the run successfully is big and bright. Hear the sounds of the skis on the snow. Feel how it will feel. Visualise it from the first-person perspective: what you will see as you ski the run, rather than merely seeing yourself skiing it.

Cause: You actually have a valid risk of danger from the run. In this situation, we are not going to mess with that fear.

Exceptional Situations

Fear of Chair Lifts

This following exercise can be used to eliminate a fear of chair lifts. It can also be used to eliminate fear of drag lifts, although, whilst fear on the chair lift is most often primarily a fear of heights, fear of drag lifts is more likely to be fear of falling and hurting yourself, or making a fool of yourself; the same powerful technique can be applied to both.

Most fears of heights stem from a single specific incident that occurred in your past. If you suffer from this, maybe you are aware of the incident – or maybe you are not. Most people do not have *any* memories before the age of about three. However, incidents which take place *prior* to that age still can affect you immensely. It is the time when a child learns the most about their environment and the most rapidly too. However, a child's understanding about their universe evolves and their memories get re-organised at about age three as they build their conceptual universe. Few remember specific incidents before that age. More often than not, any memories of earlier than age three are actually *re-constructed memories* based upon stories told by parents and photographs available.

For an example of how a one-time event could affect a person, imagine an incident where a child aged two is standing near an edge which could hurt them if they were to fall, when a distressed parent anxious about their safety shouts and screams at them for standing near the edge. The child will internalise their parent's fear while not even being fully aware of the danger they were in. However, now in adulthood, they will have no conscious recollection of the incident. Now, just thinking about heights might have their subconscious shouting and screaming at them just like their parent did: their subconscious communicating to them by giving them the same sensation of fear that their parent once did.

Luckily for us, if a single one-time event has enough power to create such a long-influencing effect on you, then another one-time event can cure it.

Exercise: "Fast Phobia" Technique to Eliminate Fears of Chair Lifts

1. Can you remember a specific time when you were scared on a chair lift? I would like you to think of a *specific* time when you were scared on a chair lift. Think about it just enough so that you start to feel some of those original feelings of fear.

2. Image yourself seated in a large empty movie theatre in front of a blank screen. Now place a black and white still image on the movie screen of the moment immediately *before* you had the fearful response for the very first time, when you were still safe, before getting on the chair lift. If you are unable to recall the very first time, instead think of the *most intense* time that you were scared in this situation.

3. Imagine leaving your body. Float out of your body and backwards, past all the empty rows of seats, and into the projection booth at the back. Stay in this projection booth until told that you can leave it.

3. Watch yourself about to watch the movie. You will see the back of yourself viewing the screen with a still image of the moment before you get on a chair lift when you are still feeling safe and secure. Keep watching yourself.

4. Play the movie in *black and white*. Play the movie of it all the way through to the end and onwards - until you reach a point of comfort and security after getting off the chair lift at the other end. Keep watching yourself watching this movie *in black and white* throughout this screening. You may notice the movie using your peripheral vision. Should you still experience vivid feelings of fear during this, make the theatre bigger and move the screen further away.

5. Freeze the frame. Once you've played the *black and white* movie to a point of security/comfort after getting off the chair lift at the other end, freeze the frame. Leave a *black and white* image on the screen of the moment where you felt safety and security again. Now, make the movie screen go completely white.

6. Leave the projection booth. Now, leave the projection booth and enter yourself watching the blank, white movie screen. Now, un-blank the movie screen so that it is showing the end *black and white* image from the movie still freeze-frozen on the screen. Change it into full *colour* image. Now actually enter the image on the movie screen itself. Fully re-associate yourself with this position of safety and security. It is as though you are in the freeze frame in full colour, through your own eyes and you are seeing what you saw then, you are hearing what you heard then.

7. Now, run the movie backwards in *colour*. Play the whole movie backwards in *colour*, at high speed so that the entire movie now only takes one and a half seconds to play - as if you were being sucked backwards in time by a giant vacuum cleaner, to arrive back at the starting point and your first position of safety and security. Make the screen go white.

8. Repeat the last step. Put yourself back at the end point of the movie without playing it, when you had comfort and security. Enter the image so you see what you saw, hear what you heard once more. Again, play the movie backwards quickly in colour so it takes just a second or so.

Keep doing this last step ten to fifteen times.

9. Check the results. Now, think of the experience again. Imagine yourself getting on the chairlift and being whisked up to the top where you get off the lift safely and in security. On a scale of 1 to 10, how would you rate your fear? If it is more than a 2, repeat the entire process from the start, taking care to do each step thoroughly, exactly as described above.

9. Confirm the results with reality. Actually get on the chairlift and check that your anxiety and fears are reduced. This is a really important step as you familiarise yourself with your new reaction (or lack of one) to being on a chair lift.

A small word of warning: *do not use this technique on any positive experiences or else the good feelings will vanish from those experiences.*

Eliminating Fears Due to Previous Injuries

Injuries can be very traumatic – both when they occur and after, when they can have long-standing influences on the psyche. If the incident was particularly painful, then injuries can easily lead to phobias simply by re-running the memories in your head over and over. Do not do that. Stop running that video! If you've had a bad trauma, realise that "once was enough".

Exercise: "Timeline" Technique to Eliminate Fears due to Previous Injuries

For this exercise, find a quiet, comfortable place where you will not be disturbed for the next ten or fifteen minutes or so. You need to be calm and relaxed for this exercise. Breathe gently and deeply through your nose. It is fine if you hear the sound of your breathing. Concentrate on the breathe entering your body, filling your chest and leaving through your mouth. Breathe like this for a few minutes.

1. Find your time line. I want you to imagine an enormous filing cabinet. Inside that filing cabinet are thousands upon thousands of folders. Each folder is either empty - and thus waiting to be filled with your future memories - or it contains a single memory of an event which you've experienced. These folders are filed in time-order sequentially, and hence contain your entire experience of life dating back from your very first memory right through to right now, with hundreds of empty folders waiting for memories from now until the moment you die. On the spine of each folders is a label of the memory within, so you know what it contains. Perhaps the label is coloured so you know at a glance which memories are happy and which ones are sad.

2. Find a folder which brings you extremely happy memories. Think of a really happy time from your past. Good. Now float above all the folders, and thumb through them until you find the folder which contains that memory. Take it out and open the folder. Look at the picture or watch the movie that is contained within. Make the image really bright and vivid. If you hear anything, make the sound really loud and clear. Make the colours really bright – and really experience the happy memory.

3. Find an empty unlabelled folder from the far future. Once your happy memory has finished playing, find an empty folder from the distance future. Open it and place into that folder *all the happy and positive emotions from the happy folder*. This is your new happy folder. Now replace the original happy folder back in its place in the cabinet.

4. Find the folder containing the traumatic event. Now, thumb through and find the folder which contains the memory of your accident. Just find

54

it. *Do not open it.* I want you to lift it out of the cabinet and put it to one side *without* opening it.

5. Preserve any valuable learning. Often, people feel that there is a part of them that thinks they should have learned something from this event. So, if there are any *learnings* from your accident which you want to preserve, very quickly take them out of the folder now, and place them in your happy folder. Make sure to leave any emotional content behind.

6. Put the happy folder into the cabinet. Slide the new happy folder back into the cabinet from the spot where you removed the last folder – the one of your accident.

7. Pick up the folder containing the memory of your accident. Imagine it starting to shrink in your hands and starting to glow brightly. As it is shrinking, it glows brighter and brighter. Soon it is a small dot, but nearly impossible to look it. It continues to shrink until all a sudden, the dot disappears and the light returns to normal.

8. Now, find the present. Thumb back through the cabinet until you find right now. Good. Now close the cabinet.

9. Check the results. Think of the accident again. On a scale of 1 to 10, how would you rate your fear?

If your fear is more than a 2, you should try the fast phobia exercise described below.

Exercise: "Fast Phobia" Technique to Eliminate Negative Emotions Caused by Traumatic Events or Injuries.

1. Can you remember a time fifteen minutes before your accident? Do *not* watch the movie yet. Just remember where it starts.

2. Image yourself seated in a large empty movie theatre in front of a blank screen. Now place a black and white still image on the movie screen of the time a few minutes *before* you had the accident, when you were still *safe* and *unhurt*.

3. Imagine leaving your body. Float out of your body and backwards, past all the empty rows of seats, and into the projection booth at the back. Stay in this projection booth until told that you can leave it.

3. Watch yourself about to watch the movie. You will see the back of yourself viewing the screen with a black and white still image of the moment before the accident when you are still feeling safe and secure. Keep watching yourself.

4. Play the movie in *black and white*. Play the movie of it all the way through to the end and onwards - until you reach a point of comfort and security. This may be moment, minutes, days or weeks after the accident. Keep watching yourself watching this movie *in black and white* throughout this screening. You may notice the movie using your peripheral vision. Should you still experience vivid feelings of fear during this, make the theatre bigger and move the screen further away. You can also make the picture smaller on the movie screen, give it a sepia tone and make it slightly fuzzy like a really old movie.

5. Freeze the frame. Once you've reach a point of security and safety after the accident, freeze the frame. Leave a *black and white* image on the screen of the moment where you felt safety and security again. Now, make the movie screen go completely white.

6. Leave the projection booth. Now, leave the projection booth and enter yourself watching the blank, white movie screen. Now, un-blank the movie screen so that it is showing the end *black and white* image from the movie still freeze-frozen on the screen. Change it into full *colour* image. Now actually *enter the image* on the movie screen itself. What you see in your head is the full colour image that was on the screen. It is no longer on the screen, but completely surrounds as you are a part of the scene itself. What you are about to hear are the sounds of the experience run backwards, loud and clear. Fully re-associate yourself with this position of safety and security. You are now freeze-frozen seeing in full colour, through your own eyes and you will be seeing what you saw then and hearing what you heard then.

7. Now, run the movie backwards from that moment in *colour*. Play the whole movie backwards in *colour*, at *extremely high speed* so that the entire movie now only takes one and a half seconds to play - as if you were being sucked backwards in time by a giant vacuum cleaner, to arrive back at the starting point and your first position of safety and security. Make the screen go white.

8. Repeat the process. Put yourself back at the end point of the movie without playing it, when you had comfort and security. Enter the image so you see what you saw, hear what you heard once more. Again, play the movie backwards fast in colour so it takes just a second or so.

Keep doing this *ten to fifteen* times.

9. Check the results. Now, think of the accident again. On a scale of 1 to 10, how would you rate your fear? If it is more than a 2, repeat the entire process from the start, taking care to do each step thoroughly, exactly as described above.

A small word of warning: *do not use this technique on any positive experiences - otherwise this will result in the good feelings vanishing from those experiences.*

Build Your Confidence

For most people, "your personal history is a set of limitations on your experience and behaviour in the present" – Bandler and Grinder.

Confidence is having belief in your abilities. In skiing, most people gradually grow their confidence as their skiing ability improves. This is a process that happens quite naturally. However, if you suffer from fear, this confidence can fail to develop as the fear gets in the way.

Luckily, there are a few techniques we can use to actually help grow your confidence. You can use your memories of previous positive experiences to prepare you for future events, and actually empower you in situations where you need those resources.

Eric knew that he'd found the beginners slopes

A lot of confidence is impaired if you have a critical and uncontrolled inner voice that does not support you. So, in this chapter, we shall teach you how to control that inner voice and turn it to your advantage, as well as how to create effective affirmations that will help you to develop that confidence naturally. You shall learn how to dissolve any limiting beliefs you have that are holding you back. You shall also learn a powerful visualisation

59

technique you can use on the slopes to build your confidence in your ability to ski any particular ski run.

Dealing with a Critical Inner Voice

We all have an inner voice. Does your inner voice tend to be encouraging, kind and upbeat? Does it make you feel good about yourself? Or does it tend to be self-critical? Does it dwell on your failures? Does it try to dishearten you?

When we ski, we often find our inner voices can get in the way.

Common Criticisms of the Inner Critic

- You'll never learn to ski

- You are too clumsy.

- You're never any good at sport.

- This slope is too steep for you.

- You are too uncoordinated to learn to ski.

- You'll never be any good.

- You made a real mess of that!

- Everyone is better than you!

There are a few things to know though:

Firstly, even if your inner voice is critical, at some level, it still actually does have *something of value* for you. We'll get to that later. However, if your inner voice is overly critical in any given situation, it would be better to have that inner voice be more encouraging and beneficial for you.

We do **not** want to silence your inner voice entirely. Some people find that just about *all* their behaviour comes from some kind of instruction or suggestion from their inner voice: "what shall I do next?", "what's the most important thing to do now"? Without that inner voice, you would be stuck in the here-and-now, completely incapacitated.

So, whilst your inner voice may criticise and taunt you, it is still an extremely valuable resource. For example, it helps you remember addresses, telephone numbers, where you left your keys, the name of the person who works downstairs. It might point out parts of the ski run you should avoid because they are difficult or even dangerous. You may have two inner voices that hold discussions to help you to make decisions: where should you go on holiday? Which restaurant should you choose? Which job should you accept. These are all examples where your inner voice is helpful.

More often than not, your inner voice does not come from our own larynx, our chest or throat. Instead, they almost always appear to come from another location, directed towards us, rather than from within.

Exercise: How to Silence Your Inner Critic

If your skiing performance is actually being impaired by your inner voice criticising you, or your motivation is reduced because your inner voice is constantly harassing you, chastising you or putting you down, then your inner voice is not really being very helpful, nor supportive of you.

Now I wonder if I can ask you to discover more about your own inner voice. The following exercise can be used to reduce the effects of that self-criticism.

1. Find its source location. Whereabouts does the voice come from? Is it behind you? In one ear? Close by or far away? Identify exactly where the source of your inner voice is located.

2. Whose voice is it? Is it your own voice? Does it sound like someone else? If is it someone else, is it someone specific?

3. How loud is the voice? Does it sound loud or quiet? What volume level is it?

4. What pitch is the voice? Is it high or low pitched?

5. Does it talk in the first-person or third-person? Does it say "I" or does it say "you"?

Being aware of your inner voice's qualities helps you to discover its structure and thus, how it has a level of power over you. In NLP terms, these are the submodalities of the voice.

Ok, now we'll play with it a little.

6. Give it a name. Call it your Gremlin. Whenever your inner voice is being critical, remember it is your Gremlin talking – not you.

7. Move the source location. Deliberately move the location where your Gremlin is speaking from. Move it so that it is located from exactly the area of your body where your own voice comes from naturally when you speak. When you move your inner voice inside your body, you might find it changes spontaneously to using "*I*" instead of "*you*". If it hasn't changed, invite it to change now, and notice how it changes your experience.

8. Turn the volume down. This will act to reduce the emotional content of its criticism.

9. Change its tonality completely. If your Gremlin is still being openly critical of your performance, change its tone. Make it sound like Mickey Mouse, Donald Duck, or Pluto.

10. Touch your larynx to anchor it. Now, whenever you hear your Gremlin being critical, touch your larynx, move its source location to where your own voice is located and change its tonality to a Disney cartoon character. Repeat this process two or three times.

One of the presuppositions of NLP is that **underlying every single behaviour there is a positive intention**. This includes your inner voice, even when it is being most critical.

So, when you hear your inner voice being critical, ask it – just as if it were an independent entity from you:

- What are you trying to accomplish for me?

- What purpose do you have in being critical of me?

- For what reason are you being critical of me?

Listen to what your voice says in reply. Common answers are:

- I don't want you to make a fool of yourself.

- I don't want you to fall over and hurt yourself.

- I want you to be the best you can be.

If you have difficulty in accepting that what your inner voice replies has a positive intention, keep asking your voice until you can find an intention that you can agree is positive.

For example, if your voice said, "You made a real mess of that", ask it in what way does that comment help you to improve your skiing. Ask it to only provide constructive criticism, and to allow you to make mistakes along your journey of learning to ski. Everyone falls when they are learning to ski.

Too often your inner critic phrases things in the negative; either linguistically stated or framed negatively. I.e. it states what is to be avoided – rather than what is to be achieved.

Ask your inner voice, "If XYZ is what you *do not* want, then what is it that you *do* want",
"how would you benefit if you were able to avoid XYZ or get rid of what you do not want?".

You might find that the purpose of the critic is to evaluate the output of the dreamer and realist as well. It is the critics job to make an analysis of the proposed behaviour to determine what exactly could go wrong, what should be avoided and bring that attention to you.

Exercise: Reframing Your Inner Voice to Support You

When your inner voice is being critical of you, you can use this exercise to help change it to being more positive and helpful for you.

1. Find the positive intention of the criticism. Ask your inner voice, "What is your positive intention?" or "How are you trying to help me by criticising me in this way?" and now listen to what your inner voice replies. Keep asking your inner voice for more information until you find a positive intention you can completely agree with.

2. Acknowledge the importance of the message. Thank your inner voice for having this positive intention for you, and acknowledge and agree with the importance of its intention.

3. Ask your inner voice to help you find some alternatives. Ask, "if there were additional ways to achieve this positive intention that were as effective as, or more effective than what it was doing, would it be willing to try them out?" Wait for a full affirmative response.

4. Call in your creativity. Ask your creativity inside to help you by finding lots and lots of alternatives that your inner voice can use to achieve its positive intention. Let your inner voice choose which ones it likes and believes will work as well as, or better than, it's previous message.

Request delayed feedback

One of the other beneficial things you can do is to ask your inner voice to *delay* giving you feedback. When you are on the piste struggling to learn, sometimes the inner voice itself is a distraction regardless of the message it is giving you; "Put your weight on the downhill leg", "Bend your knees", "Lean forward", "Control your skis".

Despite being well-meaning, too often your inner voice is reciting advice which your subconscious mind already knows anyway. Your attention then gets divided between the voice in your head and the actual sensations of skiing itself. This can lead you to actually ski the slope worse than if you did not have that "*helpful*" voice in your head.

I wonder if you will be surprised when you learn that when your inner voice is being critical on the slopes, you can ask it to give you constructive feedback and suggestions *after* you have finished that particular ski piste. You can also give it something to keep the voice occupied whilst you ski the run. Think of a tune that makes you feel confident and courageous. Now ask your inner voice to sing that tune in your head while you ski the run - and then give you feedback *only* once you have stopped at the bottom of the piste. This has the added benefit that the positive emotions you associate with the song will be triggered, thus building your confidence. Also, your inner voice will be occupied giving your subconscious a better chance to improve its skiing ability.

Dealing with Over-Generalisations

Paradoxically, over-generalisations actually narrow your view of reality as they limit your thinking to the few examples that you generalise from – thus you miss all the other possibilities.

Many people find that their inner voice has a large tendency to over-generalise.

- You never do anything right.

- You are always falling over.

- You might as well give up – You're just a failure.

- You'll never learn to ski like that.

65

- You'll never learn to use the button lift.

- I always fall over in powder.

- I am frightened of failure.

- Everybody will laugh.

All these generalisations have an "all" or a "never" in them, or an implied "forever". Linguists call such terms, *universal generalisations*.

What you can do is to *specifically* question your inner voice on the generalisation.

- "You mean there has NEVER been a time when I did anything right? Really, *never*?"

- "You mean I have always fallen over *on every single run*?"

- *For Absolute beginners:* "Surely you mean, I have not *yet* succeeded to ski a run without falling?"

- "Surely, you mean I have not *yet* learned how to successfully use the button lift?"

- "You mean I have not *yet* mastered the art of skiing powder."

- "What *exactly* are you frightened of failure to do?"

- "How do you *know* that everybody will laugh?"

When you challenge your inner voice on its generalisations, you change the context from universal situation to a specific situation. Thus, you also change the emotional content by being more positive and realistic. It acts to help prevent damage to your ego and self-esteem by forcing your inner voice to be more reasonable.

Example of dialogue with your inner voice:

"If you ski under the lift and fall, then *everyone* will laugh at you".

"Everyone in the whole world?"

"No, don't be silly. Everyone on the lift!"

"Do you really think that everyone on the lift will even be watching you? Who specifically?"

"Ok... maybe one or two".

"Is that *really* so bad?"

By challenging your inner voice on its universal generalisations, you reframe the situation and thus change your perspective on it. You should be left with a much more realistic view of the situation, and one which does not hold you back.

Eliminating Limiting Beliefs That Hold You Back

If you find that you are still unable to control your inner voice, or you are unable to break the pattern of over-generalisation, it may be that you have some fundamental beliefs that are holding you back, and your inner voice is expressing those. In which case, we need to go deeper and actually remove those limiting beliefs.

If you are being held back by your limiting beliefs, then only by changing your belief structure will you be able to progress.

Beliefs develop over time based upon your experiences. However, once your thoughts have transformed into beliefs, these ideas then become habit. They code meaning in your world, and acts as *perceptual filters* in how you view and interact with the world. "As we believe, so we experience".

Exercise: Eliminating Limiting Beliefs that Hold You Back

1. Firstly, we need to identify your limiting belief around skiing. Ask yourself, "What I believe about myself is..?" Your inner voice generalisations can give you quite a clue as to what fundamental belief you hold about yourself that is holding you back. Examples of limiting beliefs: "I cannot learn to ski because I am not sporty/athletic/too unfit/too fat", "I am too uncoordinated to ski well", "If I fall, I will probably hurt myself", "If I fall it just proves how clumsy I am". Identify the *exact* limiting belief that is holding you back: it may be a very specific belief, or quite a generalisation.

2. Identify your meta-limiting beliefs. In other words, what do you believe about that belief? Step back from the belief, and ask yourself what meaning you give to it.

3. Find out how you represent your limiting belief. It might simply be a voice in your head, said in a particular tonality, pace, loudness. It maybe that for you to believe that belief strongly, you have to hold your body in a particular way, or maybe you "feel it in your gut". If it is a visual image, then how bright is it? How intense? What clarity is the image? Try to identify exactly what you do which enforces your particular belief.

4. Identify how you represent doubts. Right, can you now think of something about which you are doubtful or unsure. What needs to happen for you to feel doubtful about anything? Is it a voice with a different pace or tonality? Do you have a different posture? Do you look in a different direction from when you are sure of something?

5. Contrast your belief and doubt representations. How do these two differ? What differences did you find between what you needed to feel the belief strongly, and what you needed to feel doubt?

6. Create a new positive belief that you would like to believe. For instance, "I am perfectly capable of learning to ski.", "If I fall, I most probably will not injure myself." Invent a new empowering belief that you would like to have in the place of your limiting belief.

8. Check the ecology of this new belief. Ask yourself, "Am I completely assured that this new belief is something I want to generate in my life?". Ask yourself, "What areas of my life will benefit from having this new belief?". If you do not get positive responses, it is best you re-think the new belief you wish to implant.

9. Transform your limiting belief into doubt. Access your limiting belief and slowly change all the submodality coding into those you have for doubt. Change the voice tonality if that is a part of how you experience belief/doubt. Change your posture if that is necessary. Consciously turn your limiting belief into doubt.

10. Flick the old limiting belief backwards and forwards between belief and doubt. Now that you have your limiting belief in the submodalities of doubt, gradually start switching your limiting belief between belief and doubt over and over. As you get the hang of this, speed it up, faster and faster and faster.

11. Implant the new empowering belief in the place of the old. Now, stop flicking your old limiting belief and leave it in the location of doubt. Think about the new empowering belief you wish to install. Switch this belief to doubt, and back and forth several times, just like before.

12. Stop with the new empowering belief encoded as belief. Turn up all the submodalities you need to fully believe your new belief. Stop, and consider what it feels like, sound like, or looks like. Amplify your new belief by making the voice louder, tonality stronger, or the image more vivid.

12. Test your beliefs. Clear your mind: think about your favourite tv show. Think about the latest news you read. Think about what you ate for breakfast. Right, now think about the subject of your old belief. What happens?

If you have successfully completed the exercise, you will no longer feel the limiting belief affecting you in the same way, and instead feel your new empowering belief.

Troubleshooting:
Cause: You still feel the limiting belief affecting you.

Solution: You may have other limiting beliefs which support the limiting belief that you wish to be rid of. If so, you should identify those other beliefs and repeat the exercise with those beliefs as well.

Another possibility is that you did not fully identify how your beliefs or doubts are represented in your system. Thus, when it came to shifting between the two representations, it was less effective as you were not fully shifting the limiting belief between belief and doubt. If so, repeat the exercise, playing particular attention to how you represent your beliefs and doubts: what exact and specific submodalities are necessary to represent those belief/doubt structures.

The Power of Affirmations

Affirmations are pithy positive statements that describe a desired situation said over and over to affirm a single thought about yourself or others. The idea is that by repeating the affirmation you convince your subconscious to allow it to become a belief.

Once you have a particular belief strongly ingrained about yourself, you naturally act accordingly with it without having to think about it.

How to create useful efficient affirmations

The greatest problem people tend to have with creating affirmations is that they create affirmations which they or their subconscious minds *cannot believe*. In other words, they are sending their subconscious contradictory messages. Consequently, they need to be very carefully phrased.

Simply saying, "I am a fantastic skier" over and over will not make it true, nor help you to learn to ski when you are just starting out and spending more time on the floor than on your skis. So do not phrase affirmations as if they have already happened. Your subconscious will only reject them.

Thus, a far better affirmation would be something which your subconscious mind can *agree with* and *believe*. For example:

"I can learn how to ski"

"Each day I can learn to ski better"

"Each day I am learning to ski better"

"Every time I ski off-piste, I learn something that helps me improve my off-piste skiing"

When you create an affirmation for yourself, check inside yourself that it is something which you can *fully believe* in. Make sure it is stated in the positive and that it is phrased in the present or future tense. Do not give it an exact deadline either.

Write your affirmations down: using a pen and pad of paper. The act of writing manually helps to firm it up in your subconscious mind.

If, when you say your affirmation, you hear your inner voice being sceptical or sarcastic or sniggering then you should carefully examine the affirmation you've chosen as it is not phrased in a manner which your subconscious will allow you to believe. Thus, it will be either completely ineffective or even boomerang back and make things worse.

Exercise: Circle of Excellence to Build Your Confidence.

The "Circle of Excellence" is an exercise you can do at home, or on the slopes. It is great exercise to do at the start of each day immediately before you put your skis on. You might like to practise this exercise regularly every time you ski. If so, do not be surprised when you notice how you have feelings of confidence every time you step into your skis, perhaps sooner than you'd expect.

I suggest you might like to read the exercise through once before trying it out.

I wonder if you can remember a specific time when you felt a really strong, total, inner sense of confidence. It can be totally unrelated to skiing – just pick a really strong, vivid memory which you will enjoy remembering.

1. Feel that confidence once again. There's really no need to "take a deep breath and close your eyes" – but you can if it helps you get back into the same state of confidence. Let yourself go back to that moment when you felt fully 100% confident. Re-live that exact moment in your mind, seeing exactly what you saw, hearing exactly what you heard and feeling exactly how you felt. Re-create the posture you had at that moment. Breathe in and out at the same rate. Feel the confidence of that moment surging now within you again.

Make the pictures in your mind of that moment really vivid. Picture it in high definition, with the colours really bright. Turn the volume up on the sound to really intensify the memory.

2. Circle of Excellence. Now, as you feel your confidence-level building within you, imagine a coloured circle on the floor around your feet getting wider and wider as your inner confidence grows. What colour would you like the circle to be? Does it emit a sound that indicates how powerful it is? When the circle is at its largest and your feelings of confidence are greatest, *step out* of that circle on the ground, leaving those feelings of confidence within the circle. This request is rather unusual, and you can do it.

3. Imagine yourself just about to put your skis on. Your ski boots are on, your ski jacket cosy around you and you are just about to put your skis on. Your skis are lying flat on the snow, parallel to each other with space around them. It is just before your first ski run of the day.

4. Centre your circle of excellence on your skis. Now imagine your circle of excellence surrounds your skis; its centre exactly halfway between each ski situated near the bindings. See the colour of the circle exactly as before; hear the noise that it is making. As soon as you can strongly visualise this circle around your skis, step into it, and click into your ski bindings. Check your bindings are firm. Imagine yourself with your skis on, now surrounded by your circle of excellence, with those same feelings of confidence fully available to you.

Exercise: Teach Your Subconscious to Ski with *Phantom-self* skiing.

Now, I would like you to have a new experience. This is an advanced visualisation exercise that you can practise either at home curled up on the sofa, or more productively, in the field, standing at the top of a real ski slope.

When done successfully, this is an example of a positive hallucination designed to help teach your subconscious how to ski. It works by preparing your subconscious for the skiing experience before you actually ski the slope. The advantage of conducting such visualisation before is that it actually helps prepare you for the experience with the complete absence of fear.

Part one:

I want you to see yourself standing at the top of the slope. Are you seeing that? Great!

Now imagine yourself *floating out of your own body* on skis, and visually-imagine your phantom-self setting off down the slope, skiing absolutely perfectly. See your phantom-self bend perfectly into each turn, being in total control. Imagine your phantom-self using the terrain itself to control their speed with a pace at which you feel comfortable and in control. Your phantom-self skier experiences no fear.

I want you to image exactly what your phantom-self will hear; the *sound* of the snow sliding beneath their skis; how the sound changes when they turn, when they speed up just a little, when they slow down. Image how it will *feel* to them through their skis and boots as they ski down the slope. Imagine exactly how the snow feels under their skis through their boots – the undulations of the snow, how it feels crossing the little lines if the piste is immaculately groomed.

Imagine your phantom-self skiing calmly; easily controlling the turns, *enjoying* the experience. Guide your phantom-self *successfully* all the way down, and bring them to a controlled stop at the bottom of the slope.

Great. Now bring them back up the slope and back inside you.

Part two:

Set your phantom-self off skiing down the slope once again.

Wait until they do their first turn. Now this time, I want you to imagine exactly how it will *look* like from *their perspective*; through their eyes, from their point of view. What will the terrain beneath their feet look like as they ski down the slope? What does it look like through their eyes?

You are now inside your own phantom-self skiing down the slope.

Again, image how it will *sound* with the snow sliding beneath your skis; how the sound changes when you turn. Image how it will *feel* through your skis and boots.

Guide your phantom-self all the way down the slope and bring yourself to a controlled stop at the bottom of the slope.

Brilliant.

Can you now imagine *and realise* that you are perfectly capable of skiing down that slope too, just as your phantom-self just managed it. In actual fact, it was YOU that successfully managed to control your phantom-self skiing down the slope.

Part three:

Ski!

Creating a Winning Attitude

"You cannot teach a man anything; You can only help him discover it within himself" – Galileo Galilei

Learning to ski can take some time and effort, and everyone learns at a different pace, however there is a science to creating a positive attitude of achievement. After NLP trainer, Gray Faris, was involved in a severe accident, he intensively studied what successful athletes do to rehabilitate following injuries: trying to find the core characteristics of those who recover successfully. He found that there are six characteristics that guaranteed a winning attitude.

Inner Motivation

For maximum gain, it really helps to have an inner motivation: A burning desire to succeed with compelling visions of what you want to achieve.

There are two types of goal:

- Those that work by the power of attraction – an example of a positively framed goal around getting fit for skiing might be *"Be a lean, mean skiing machine"*.

- Those that work by the power of repulsion – or rather, away from unpleasant circumstances. For example, *"Ski a whole run without stopping to catch my breath"*.

The best athletes and consequently skiers use both of these types of goal to build their inner motivation. They vividly imagine very specific desirable and worthwhile goals that attract them, and also, vividly imagine the worst circumstances if they were not to achieve them.

Anthony Robbins calls this "the Dickens scenario" - where you associate massive pain to the consequences of not changing now, and you associate massive pleasure to the experience of changing now.

When you pick your goals, you should try to ensure that they have the following characteristics:

They should be:

Specific
Measurable
Attractive
Realistic
Time phrased.

Ideas for suitable goals might be:

- Master starting and stopping in a controlled manner in a straight line on a gentle nursery slope

- Master the snowplough turn

- Ski my first blue run

- Ski confident parallel turns on blue runs

- Enjoy skiing red runs

- Enjoy skiing moguls or bumps

- Ski my first black run in total confidence

For more on how to set effective goals, see the appendix.

Chunking down goals

It is easier to learn one discrete skill at a time.

Rather than aiming to ski the whole slope in one go, instead, pick a spot on the slope just 30 metres below you – aim to ski to there under control, rather than ski the entire mountain. Then repeat ad infinitum, until you are down the mountain.

If your goal is to "*ski a red run*", and you have only just started learning to ski, rather than attack the blues and the red runs, learn to control yourself on the smaller, less steep, beginners slopes. Gain your confidence there. Practise your technique until it is habitual and automatic. Practise, practise,

practise... and then move onto the next level.   Ask a much more experienced skier than you to watch you ski, to see if you are ready for a more challenging slope. And then, progress slowly. Remember not all blue slopes are the same. Some are harder than others. Get advice.

Remember the following advice:

- Avoid ski slopes that are beyond your abilities.

- Stop well before you become excessively tired.

- Be realistic about the consequences of a fall.

- Talk yourself down slopes that you know you are able to ski

- Remember to take some time often - to look around and enjoy your surroundings.

High Standards

Rather than simply want to ski without feeling afraid, you should aim to actually ski with confidence – after all, it is about enjoying yourself! You should not be content with simply getting down the slope alive. Instead, aim to get down the slope in style, under control, and feeling good and confident.

By setting high standards for yourself, you raise the level of the game. Realise right now that if you do not have the technical ability just yet, then you will acquire it as you progress and become more experienced. This leads nicely to the next characteristic...

Flexible time frame

Everybody learns at a different rate. Consequently, be patient: It will come.   Experience your present situation fully and get involved with improving your ability to ski. Think about the improvements you will make and enjoy those in the present.   Enjoy the learning process. Concentrate on learning the basics really well. Spending an extra day or so on a green run practising your snowplough technique is nothing compared to the setback that could occur if you push ahead onto the next level before you are ready for it!

Even as an advanced skier, when I feel I am having a bad day, I will often ski a few runs that I know I always enjoy and can ski well. This breaks my state from being depressed about having a poor performance, and gets me reconnected with skiing well. If you find that you are consistently not skiing up to the level you normally ski, relax, go have a coffee, think about the times you were skiing really well. Practise some of the exercises from the chapter, "Achieve Peak Performance".

If your inner voice is saying, "Gosh. All my friends are much better – or learning much quicker than me – or they are all on blue runs and I am stuck on a green", then do some of the exercises from the chapter, "Build your Confidence" on how to control your inner voice. Remember that learning to ski is not a competition – and do not rush the learning process.

Get personally involved

You are completely responsible for your own body. Thus you are completely responsible for your own ability to learn to ski. So accept responsibility for it and get involved.

If you fall over, it is not just something that happened *to* you. Everything has a cause. Falling over is the effect – although you may not be consciously aware of *exactly* why you fell. Normally when skiing you fall because your body was unbalanced; perhaps you caught an edge of a ski or you were not paying attention to the snow fully, or you tried to ski outside of the rules of physics. Avoid thinking of yourself as a passive participant. When you accept responsibly for your own ability to learn to ski, you also accept responsibility for both your actions and inactions.

Only make self-to-self comparisons

Above all, never compare yourself to anyone better than yourself. Look solely at your own progress and compare yourself to that.

"Anyone who has ever tried, learned and then mastered a sport, a profession or a musical instrument knows that countless failures are at the base of any success" – Andreas and Faulkner.

Here in Chamonix at the foot of Western Europe's highest mountain, Mont-Blanc, where we run a ski chalet, it is a "Mecca" for extreme sports. Lots of professional extreme skiers live here; drawn by the amazing off-piste available in the mountains, drawn by the most extreme routes.

Consequently, what I have learnt is: *there is always a better skier!* This is true at just about any level. There are people in Chamonix doing amazing death-defying descents, skiing routes and lines and places that make me breathless just thinking about it.

Comparing ourselves to anyone else is only truly valuable when it shows us *what is possible* to achieve. Even then, it is only useful if it also serves as a valuable model on *how to achieve it*. Use it only as inspiration to motivate you.

Never compare yourself with where you *expected* yourself to be. Expectation can be a cruel master of disappointment. Instead, gain a sense of achievement, and a genuine sense of progress, by *only* comparing where you are *now* with your skiing, to where you were on day one when you did not even know how to put your skis on. If you *are* an absolute beginner on day one and struggling, remember that yesterday you were not even a beginner.

Achieving Peak Performance

"What are you waiting for? You're faster than this. Don't think you are, know you are. Come on! Stop trying to hit me and hit me!" - Morpheus from The Matrix.

NLP provides a technique to enables you to reproduce *any state you wish* simply by creating an anchor to that state, which you then trigger whenever you desire to re-experience that state of being.

After he'd anchored his peak performance,
Eric knew he was unstoppable!

Ivan Pavlov discovered the principle behind anchors when he studied laboratory dogs. He observed that the dogs salivated when they smelled meat powder. He then rang a bell whenever the dogs were exposed to the meat powder. Very soon, he found that the dogs would salivate when just the bell was rung. He called this a *"conditioned reflex"*. This same principle of *classical conditioning* affects humans too.

An anchor can be a touch, a sound, a word or phrase. It can be a look or a smell or a taste. It is simply a sensory stimulus which is *linked* to a specific set of *emotional states*.

For example, have you ever had a really bad job? One that you really disliked? Did you ever find that *merely entering* the building where you worked would make you feel depressed? Your depressed feeling was *anchored* to entering the building.

Is there someone you really love and when anyone merely mentions their name, you feel really good inside? In this case, feeling really good (*emotional state*) is anchored to hearing your loved one's name (*specific auditory stimulus*).

These are all examples of anchored experiences: The smell of a fantastic Sunday roast dinner which triggers your feelings of warmth, happiness, and a great appetite. Hearing your favourite piece of music which makes you instantly relax – or get excited.

Anchoring Your Successful Experiences

Most people travel through life allowing anchors to be created subconsciously and never control *what* they allow to affect them, nor *how* it affects them. However, you can also create and use anchors *consciously* to allow you to access your most productive states.

Now you already know how to create anchors. You have been creating anchors all your life. So, let us look at how you go about doing this consciously to allow you to consistently *achieve peak performance* for your skiing....

Exercise: Anchoring Your Peak Performance

This exercise should be done on the slopes for maximum benefit; *immediately* after you have had a really fantastic experience whilst skiing.

1. Establish the successful resourceful state that you wish to anchor

Let's say you've just skied **better** than you ever have before...

Maybe it was your first green run without falling over.
Maybe it was your best run flying down through waist-deep powder.

You still are feeling that warm glow of success; that joyful self-satisfaction that comes with a great ski run; an achievement. You are pleased and proud of yourself. Notice how you are feeling about your experience of skiing that particular run.

What if after *every* ski run you could feel this way?
How much *quicker* could you improve if you *started* each ski run in this empowering neurophysiological state?

2. Immediately create the anchor

Assuming you have poles, jab them vertically down into the snow either side of your skis, whilst cheering the word, "YES!!!" Say it out LOUD and with true passion. You've just experienced your best run so you will already be feeling invigorated and joyful – let your feelings explode out with a joyful, happy, passionate, congratulatory "YES"!

This will create what is known in NLP terms as an **anchor**.

You've just a created an anchor to the neurophysiological state you were in when you finished that last ski run – and consequently created an anchor to your most resourceful skiing state! Note: You should try to create anchor immediately you finish the ski run as if you wait until the peak has passed, you may anchor the decline in your intense state.

Note: If you are a beginner and not using poles – or a snowboarder - then you could, for example, clap your hands together strongly whilst cheering "Yes!" with passion. What is important here is not the specific motion, but merely that it should be a *unique reproducible action*.

I like to create positive anchors using my ski equipment such as the jabbing movement with my poles described above, or my personal favourite, the mere act of clicking my boots into my bindings. I've anchored my most resourceful state for skiing – being simultaneous calm, clear of mind, confident and being slightly aggressive in my skiing - into the mere act of putting my skis on!

You do not even have to shout "Yes!" as part of the anchor.
I include it in the exercise simply as it provides a powerful additional

auditory stimulus for the anchor. You can create an anchor to just about any unique action – it can be discreet like the poles jab or clicking into your skis, or loud like a shout or cheer. It just needs to be unique.

3. Reinforce your anchor

Anchors that are not reinforced soon fade – thus reinforcement is an essential part of the process. Also be aware that if you practise this exercise at home *beforehand*, you will probably need to re-anchor the experience when you are on the slopes themselves for immediacy, so that the exercise is effective.

So, whenever you have a *successful* ski run again and are experiencing the same feelings of happiness and success, repeat the process in *exactly* the same manner. Slap your arm in the same place with the same force. Jab the snow with your poles and say "Yes!" once more with the same level of passion. This will reinforce your anchor and build its strength.

The idea is to create a strong positive anchor that you can use to transport yourself *immediately* back to the resourceful state of your successful run.

4. How to use your anchor

Now, the situation arises where you would like to be in that same powerful resourceful state *before* you begin your next ski run.

Perhaps it is the first run of the day? An unknown or difficult run? Maybe you are feeling a little apprehensive? A little nervous, perhaps? A steep slope you've never skied before?

What is important is that **being in that powerful positive resourceful state would enable you to ski the run ahead at your peak performance.**

Time to bring out the new weapon in your mental arsenal.

Repeat your anchor now – Jab the snow and cheer "Yes!" before you start, and notice how your feelings immediately change. Notice how you are feeling more excited, more confident and exuberant. Ready to ski! Notice how your feelings have morphed into being the same as your previous successful ski run that you anchored.

Right, ready, set, ski! Enjoy!

Troubleshooting

If you don't get the same positive feelings of your anchor, it might mean one of the following common problems:

Cause: Your fears and anxious anticipation of the skiing ahead is getting in the way of your positive anchor. I.e. Your current negative emotions are way stronger than the positive emotions of the anchor.

Solution: When you feel a level of fear or anxiety about the ski run ahead, *first*, practise some of the exercises on fear from the previous chapters to reduce your fears and anxiety *before* you fire your positive anchor.

Note: you might find that firing your positive anchor even once whilst your negative feelings are stronger will act to dissolve the effectiveness of your positive anchor for future firings. If that is the case, you need to re-create and re-build the strength of your positive anchor.

Cause: Your positive anchor might be too weak or not 'positive' enough.

Solution: You should re-anchor a more powerful and more positive emotional experience. You need to be feeling in a really positive resourceful state immediately as you create the anchor in order for it to be firmly established.

Final Thoughts

Always be positive: Do not fear falling or failing. See every fall as an opportunity to learn and embrace them. I have a personal motto: "*If you do not fall, you are **not trying hard enough**!*".

Reflect on your progress: Look back at the beginners slopes and recognise your progress. Be proud of yourself for learning to ski. Be proud of your progress and achievement.

Never compare yourself to anyone else: Everyone learns at a different pace. Everyone has different "natural" abilities. Consequently, never compare yourself to anyone else. Also, try not to have expectations about how quickly you will learn.

Get the basics right: Practise, practise, practise. Learn a confident snow plough before moving onto parallel turns. Practise your parallel turns so you are confident in them on all degrees of slope – then only progress to more difficult slopes when your ability and confidence are able. Get your jump turns sorted and ensure your fitness before you attempt long steeps.

And one final question: having read this book through and done the exercises relevant to your fears, how surprised will you feel when you get on the ski slope and find that you now *allow yourself to feel much more calm and confident skiing*?

Appendix

How to set effective goals

When you create a goal with the following traits – *specific, measurable, attractive, realistic and time-phased* - they help you to focus on what you want to achieve in ways which psychologically improve your ability to see the goal through. Nevertheless, there are a few traits which are not part of the acronym, but which are equally important if you are trying to set really effective goals! It is possible to create SMART goals which fail to create enough psychological engagement with your goal, and also fail to take aspects of your own psychological constitution into account.

If you craft your goal correctly, both in how your goal is worded, and what it is about, then it becomes a springboard for the motivation and commitment you need to bring that goal to fruition.

Your goal should be:

Specific

Your goal should be specific. This means that the goal is clearly identified, and free from ambiguity. It should have a *tightly defined outcome*. For example, "Ski much better" is not specific enough. How much better? Over what time period? For what purpose? How are you going to tell when you have achieved it?

By making your goal specific, you really nail what the goal is about in your own mind – which allows your psychological processes to kick in and help you bring it into reality. It helps allow your "reticular activating system" – those brain cells that filter perception – to bring opportunities to your attention, and help you become more aware of your behaviour in situations that affect how you achieve your goal.

Measurable

Your goal should be measurable. By introducing some element of measurability into your goal, you can be much more aware and informed of your progress with the goal. Again, it allows you to have much stronger and reliable feedback. Also, by making your goal measurable, it generally helps with increasing how specific the goal is.

It should be noted that with some goals, the measurability can be whether the goal "event" has actually happened, or not. For example, if your goal is to "Ski the Vallée Blanche in Chamonix valley" then the element of measurability here is simply whether you did, or did not. With other goals, the measurability is much clearer – for example, "Ski the entire blue piste past the chalet in control and in under four minutes thirty seconds". Here, the measurability also allows you to chart your progress, which is an excellent feedback tool.

Attractive

If your goal is not desirable to you, if you aren't attracted to your goal, then how can you become effectively motivated towards achieving it? The best goals are ones which literally have you leaping out of bed in the morning to complete. They get you excited and inspired. Attractive, desirable goals maintain a high interest level for you in attaining your outcome. They keep you emotionally engaged with the end result that you desire: your goal's completion.

The best goals aren't wishes. They aren't wants. The very best goals stem from desires so deep and strong that they attract you at such a core level that the meaning you attribute to their completion becomes ingrained within your very personality – basically, completing the goal then becomes an expression of *who you are*.

The most effective goals are ones which most explicitly express your values. This is because when you realise those goals, they become an expression of *who you actually are*, rather than being an expression of something you are striving for, or even something you merely would like.

Effective goals are often goals which have an element of creativity in how they are worded. It is this creativity which can help make them inspiring to you because they engage different parts of your brain when you read or think of them. A goal which is worded in a bland or ordinary fashion does little to excite you, whereas the same goal worded in an interesting and exciting manner can really help keep you focussed and interested in the goal.

For example:

bland goal = *Lose 8 kgs*
juicy goal = *Be a lean, mean, skiing machine*

bland goal = *Ski a mogul field without falling*
juicy goal = *Looking good and feeling fine with moguls* *

bland goal = *Ski a red run*
juicy goal = *Celebrate my BIG win skiing a red piste with a Champagne and Strawberries party*

The trick to introducing creative elements into your goal is to find the words and phrases that are really exciting and interesting *to you*. The exact elements which will give your goal that extra sparkle and magic will depend entirely on your own psychology. It is up to you not to be lazy, instead take some extra time designing goals which will keep your interest levels really high, design goals which will keep you psychologically engaged with them.

When you design your goal correctly, it will suddenly *feel* more exciting to you. It will appear more attractive to you, and start to get you feeling much more motivated towards taking action. You will literally want to get started NOW.

* If you are wondering *where* the measurability of goals like this comes in, sometimes it is better to discard the measurability within the phrasing of the goal in favour of increase attractiveness. You can re-introduce measurability easily, for example, by asking yourself, *"On a scale of 1-10, how confident do I feel skiing this mogul field?"* both at the start and at the end of the time period.

Realistic

Do you have the time, talent, resources and commitment to achieving this goal? If not, are you being realistic in setting such a goal for yourself? If you've only just started skiing, then it is unrealistic to expect to be able to ski off-piste by the end of the week!

One person's "achievable" is another person's pipedream, so you do have to be very aware of your own capabilities. Often times though, people can perform well in excess of what they would normally expect when they have the support, and encouragement of others who want to see them succeed. You need to strike a balance between goals that are too small to get you motivated, and goals where you are simply setting yourself up for failure.

What is realistic *can* also be a factor of what society has *conditioned you to believe* as being realistic though – and it is interesting when those paradigms are broken. In 1983, an unknown 61 year old farmer, Cliff Young, ran 875kms in less than 6 days to win the Sydney – Melbourne ultra-marathon race, beating world-class athletes by over six hours. For most people, it is not really realistic to believe that an unknown person of that age could win such a race, but it provides a wonderful example of just how the power of one's beliefs can affect just what may appear to be "realistic".

Time phased

When you give your goal a target date for completion, you do two things. Firstly, it acts as a structure which helps you develop strategies for its completion. For example, the strategies to learn to ski off-piste may be very different if the time period for its completion is either one week, or one month. The second thing is, it creates a *sense of urgency* over its completion. Instead of merely talking about what you want to do, having a time period helps spur you into action because you start to think about *when* things need to happen.

Having a target date for completion also helps you to evaluate exactly where you are in relation to completing the goal. Thus, it helps provide you with a feedback mechanism and a means to measure or chart your progress.

Creating a time frame, of course, is much easier if you have a skiing goal and go on just one skiing holiday per year!

Positively phrased

Always ensure that your goal is phrased in a positive manner. Your brain is wired towards creating what you DO want, rather than avoiding what you don't. In addition, positively phrased goals then become much more inspiring, and fun – instead of being about fixing some aspect of yourself, positively phrased goals are about extending and enhancing yourself.

Try to avoid creating goals with words like "stop, quit, lose, don't". Think about the positive things you gain by your goal. Ask yourself what you *gain* by achieving the goal. Aim at where you *want to be*, rather than where you don't want to be.

For example, a positively phrased version of "lose 15 pounds of weight" might be "gain a svelte toned figure". Instead of "stop telling myself I cannot ski" a more positive phrased version might be "enjoy my new self-image as a competent skier having a great time on the slopes".

Challenging

A challenging goal will bring out the best of your performance. A challenging goal will demand for you to extend yourself, your capabilities and beliefs. It will ask for you to be a better person tomorrow than you are today – in a whole host of different ways. A challenging goal gives you something to aspire to, as well as a strong focal point for you to aim your energy.

Challenges help you to discover things about yourself that you never really knew before, and by setting out to achieve them, they enable you to rise to produce a superior performance.

Inspiring

For a goal to really be effective, it is necessary that you find the outcome inspiring in some way. The best goals leave you slightly nervous and excited at the prospect of achieving them. When the goal inspires you, it gives you energy and purpose, which will help drive you onwards towards success when obstacles appear.

Congruous with your values and integrity

Most people create goals that are congruous with their integrity because it *automatically* creates psychological discomfort if they don't, but perhaps the biggest error is to create goals which contradict your values structure. Basically, values are the set of emotional states that you wish to feel on a regular basis. Examples of values include: adventure, comfort, security, health, love, family, prosperity. People struggle with their goals, for example, if they create an exercise goal, but then value comfort more than feeling healthy.

The solution is to be very clear about what values you currently have, and what values it will take to achieve your goal, and then actually alter the things you value in life. Once you actually know what your current values are, together with how you prioritise them, you can mentally choose to change and alter the priority you place upon them – or even discard them altogether. By then reinforcing your new values structure with your new behaviours, you can gradually change the way you experience life. You can do this because you can actually decide which emotional states are important to you, and the priority you place upon them – it's a choice.

Exercise: Build your Motivation to Get Fit Before Your Ski Holiday

1.   Current Situation. You know getting fit before your skiing holiday would greatly benefit you whilst you are away, but you never seem to get around to actually exercising.

2.   Check For Any Objections. Ask yourself, does any part of you have any *valid* objections to you actually getting fitter before your skiing holiday? Do you have any valid heart conditions? Are you obese? If so, you should see a doctor before starting your get fit programme.

3.   "Dickens" scenario. Think about the results you will obtain if you **do not** get fit for skiing: for example: feeling tired too soon, completing fewer runs in the day, having to stop too soon to simply re-catch your breath. Not being able, or strong enough, to ski the runs you wish. Not being able to keep up with the other members of your party.

4.   Change your feelings to the "Dickens". Think about the results you do *not* want to obtain. Make these images WAY darker, slower and heavier and more ugly. Change them in your head to make them *really unpleasant* for you. For example; panting every few metres to catch your breath, falling over with utter exhaustion, being embarrassed and utterly appalled by your ski fitness, being left behind whilst your friends ski without you.

5.   Rewards and Consequences. Now think about the end benefits of what getting fit for skiing would mean to you – not the actual process of getting fit - but the *joy* and *positive benefits* you would gain through actually being fantastically fit for skiing before your ski holiday happens. Imagine yourself flying down the runs, feeling fit and strong. Having your "ski legs" from day one! Impressing your ski friends with your new-found level of fitness.

5.   Change your feelings to the situation. Think about the fitness results you *want* to obtain. Imagine yourself flying down the ski runs feeling healthy, fit and vibrant. Make these images bigger and brighter and stronger and louder. More colourful. More vivid. Add voices of encouragement and cheers, making the prospect of getting fit more and more attractive and compelling until you feel motivated to get started now.

6. Take action immediately. Take some action. Any action. Right now. Go exercise! Research how to get fit for skiing. Purchase a "fitness for skiing" book. Get a coach. Book a session with a fitness instructor. Whatever... just GO DO IT RIGHT NOW!

Advice for Ski Instructors wanting to use NLP.

Establish a resource anchor. Ask the client to close their eyes and think of a really happy specific memory; a time when they felt really safe and secure. Confirm that they are thinking of this safe, happy memory. When they say yes, get them to describe the event in lots of vivid detail, running the movie through in their head. Get them to make it bigger and brighter – fully associate into it. Now, while the client is in such a great, resourceful, neurophysiological state, anchor it kinaesthetically by squeezing one of their shoulders with a firm grip. You can use this resource anchor to help re-establish a resourceful, safe and secure state in your client when necessary.

Layer your resource anchors. Get the client to reflect upon a time when they felt completely *confident*. Again, have them relive it. Get them to amplify the experience, and when it is at the peak of intensity, you say, for example, "Right.... let's *ski!*" in a particular tone of voice at the same time.

How to create a super-resourceful state: When you are about to take the client down a run where you know they would normally be very fearful, trigger both these anchors at the same time – squeeze their shoulder in exactly the spot, in the same manner whilst saying "Right.... let's *ski!*" using the same tone of voice from the second anchor. It will trigger both their confident and safe and secure states simultaneously.

Breaking Someone's Fear Strategy

When the client is in an un-resourceful state, you need to *break the strategy* of their emotional experience: Preferable with something which makes them laugh. You can shout, grip their arm, move their chin so they are now looking at you, basically do something *completely unexpected*: tell them to burp – do *anything* which breaks their fear strategy.

Another way to break someone's strategy is to invoke a *meta-state*. Not only can you feel anxious, but you can feel ridiculous about feeling so anxious. You can have states about your state.

97

You can stop your client when they are showing signs of fear, and ask them, "*and how do you feel about being afraid?*". This acts to disassociate them from the fear itself and regard it separately from themselves. These meta-states can be used to then modify the original state. A meta-state can become as intense as the original state: it then replaces the original state and becomes the primary state for the client. For instance, get them to feel a little angry about being afraid. For some, this will act as a motivator to overcome their fears.

Also, if you can get them to elicit exactly how they create their fear response, then you can give them a level of control over it. You can get them to *break their own strategy* when they feel fear is impairing their performance.

Magic with Linguistics

Use tenses appropriately to put a problem in the past. "That has been a problem, hasn't it?" rather than "That is a problem isn't it."

Say:

"How incredible that you always remember to feel afraid when you look at a ski piste! I can't even remember to take out the trash. You actually remember to feel afraid every time you see a ski piste. Wow! Amazing! If you can learn to feel afraid from a one-time experience, you can unlearn it from another one-time experience, right?"

Bibliography

Andreas, Steve; Faulkner, Charles. (1996) – "**NLP, The New Technology of Achievement**". Harper Paperbacks.

Bandler, Richard. (1993) – "**Time for a Change**". Meta Publications.

Bandler, Richard; Grinder, John. (1979) – "**Frogs into Princes**". Real People Press.

Bandler, Richard; Grinder, John; Delozier, Judith. (1975) – "**Patterns of the Hypnotic Techniques of Milton Erickson, MD, volume II**". Grinder & Associates.

Bodenhamer, Bob G.; Hall, Michael L. (2001) – "**The User's Manual for the Brain**". Crown House Publishing.

Dilts, Robert. (1999) – "**Sleight of Mouth: the magic of conversational belief change**". Meta Publications.

Dilts, Robert; Hallbom, Tim; Smith, Suzi. (1990) – "**Beliefs – Pathways to Health and Well-being**". Metamorphous Press.

Erickson, Milton H.;   Rossi, Ernest L. (1979) – "**Hypnotherapy – An Exploratory Casebook**". New York. Irvington Publishers.

Gallway, Timothy W; Kriegel, Robert. (1997) – "**Inner Skiing**". Random House.

Hall, Michael L. (1996) – "**The Spirit of NLP: The Process, Meaning, and Criteria for Mastering NLP**". The Anglo American Book Company.

Hall, Michael L.; Belnap, Barbara P. (1999) – "**The Sourcebook of Magic – A Comprehensive Guide to the Technology of NLP**". Crown House Publishing Limited,

James, Tad. (cassette) – "**Introducing The Art And Science of Time Line Therapy Techniques**". Advanced Neuro Dynamics, Inc.

James, Tad; Woodsmall, Wyatt. (1988) –"**Timeline therapy and the Basis Of Personality**". Meta Publications.

O'Connor, Joseph. (2001) – "**NLP Workbook: A Practical Guide to Achieving the Results You Want**". Thorsons.

Robbins, Anthony. (1991) – "**Awaken the Giant Within**". New York: Simon & Schuster.

Robbins, Anthony. (1986) – "**Unlimited Power: The New Science of Personal Achievement**". New York: Simon & Schuster.

Vaknin, Shlomo. (2008) – "**The Big Book of NLP Techniques: 200+ Patterns, Method & Strategies of Neuro Linguistic Programming**". BookSurge Publishing.

Final note – spread the word

Here's what you can do to spread the word about "Skiing without Fear".

1. Loan this book to a friend who skis who has issues with fear and building their skiing confidence.

2. Send them a link to http://www.skiing-without-fear.com where they can download it an eBook copy themselves or purchase the hard copy version, or audio book.

3. Sign up and join the discussion on http://www.skiing-without-fear.com

Good Luck!
Let me know how you get on: leighton@skiing-without-fear.com

One final note: *if you are interested in having a fantastic ski holiday in a catered ski in, ski out chalet in Chamonix, France run by the author and his wife, with fabulous gourmet food, hot tub, log fire, multimedia entertainment system, then do check us out and come stay with us at Chalet Maison Jaune.*

Full details here: http://www.maison-jaune.com

Skiing Without Fear

5244520R00058

Printed in Great Britain
by Amazon.co.uk, Ltd.,
Marston Gate.